International Summit on the Teaching Profession

# Teaching Excellence through Professional Learning and Policy Reform

## LESSONS FROM AROUND THE WORLD

Andreas Schleicher

This work is published under the responsibility of the Secretary-General of the OECD. The opinions expressed and arguments employed herein do not necessarily reflect the official views of the OECD member countries.

This document and any map included herein are without prejudice to the status of or sovereignty over any territory, to the delimitation of international frontiers and boundaries and to the name of any territory, city or area.

**Please cite this publication as:**
Schleicher, A. (2016), *Teaching Excellence through Professional Learning and Policy Reform: Lessons from Around the World,* International Summit on the Teaching Profession, OECD Publishing, Paris.
*http://dx.doi.org/10.1787/9789264252059-en*

ISBN 978-92-64-25204-2 (print)
ISBN 978-92-64-25205-9 (PDF)

Series: International Summit on the Teaching Profession
ISSN 2312-7082 (print)
ISSN 2312-7090 (online)

The statistical data for Israel are supplied by and under the responsibility of the relevant Israeli authorities. The use of such data by the OECD is without prejudice to the status of the Golan Heights, East Jerusalem and Israeli settlements in the West Bank under the terms of international law.

**Photo credits:**
© AsiaPix/Inmagine
© Jose Luis Pelaez, Inc./Blend Images/Corbis

Corrigenda to OECD publications may be found on line at: *www.oecd.org/publishing/corrigenda*.

# Foreword

The skills that students need to contribute effectively to society are changing constantly, but school systems are not keeping up. Most schools look much the same today as they did a generation ago, and many teachers feel insufficiently prepared to develop the practices and skills required to meet the diverse needs of today's learners.

To build teacher professionalism, policy makers and the profession itself must establish clearly and concisely what teachers are expected to know and be able to do. Many of the key attributes and skills of successful teachers will only become evident once teachers begin working in the classroom. Formal, measurable skills are necessary but not sufficient; they must be complemented by the intangible qualities that are difficult to quantify, including motivation and self-efficacy. And these qualities are often enhanced as teachers improve their performance and effectiveness through professional development activities – and as education systems recognise teachers' professionalism.

These things are easy to say, but hard to do. It is rarely possible to predict clear, identifiable links between education policies and outcomes, especially given the lag involved between the time at which the initial cost of reform is incurred, and the time when it is evident whether the intended benefits of reforms actually materialise. As a result, there are a lot of stakeholders in education who have a vested interest in maintaining the status quo. Even small reforms can involve massive reallocations of resources, and touch the lives of millions on both the client and provider sides. This makes it essential to build broad political support for any proposed reform. In essence, education reform will not happen unless educators endorse and implement it.

To help governments make education reform happen, while placing teachers and school leaders at the centre of improvement efforts, the German ministers of education, the OECD and Education International brought education ministers, union leaders and other teacher leaders together for the sixth International Summit on the Teaching Profession in Berlin, Germany, in March 2016.

One of the secrets of the success of the International Summit on the Teaching Profession is that it explores difficult and controversial issues on the basis of sound evidence, provided by the OECD as global leader for internationally comparable data and analysis. This publication summarises the evidence that underpins the 2016 summit, bringing together data analysis and experience to develop better education policies for better lives.

The report was prepared by Andreas Schleicher, based on data and comparative analysis from several OECD publications: "How teachers teach and students learn: Strategies for success at school" (forthcoming), *Supporting Teacher Professionalism: Insights from TALIS 2013* (2016); *TALIS 2013 Results: An International Perspective on Teaching and Learning* (2014); *Synergies for Better Learning: An International Perspective on Evaluation and Assessment* (2013); *Creating Effective Teaching and Learning Environments: First Results from TALIS* (2009); and *Teachers Matter: Attracting, Developing and Retaining Effective Teachers* (2005).

Karine Tremblay provided expert advice, Marilyn Achiron edited the text, and Sophie Limoges co-ordinated production of the report.

# Table of Contents

BOXES



FIGURES

TABLES

# Executive Summary

Today's teachers need to prepare students for jobs that have not yet been created, to use technologies that have not yet been invented, and to solve social problems that haven't arisen before. Teachers have to do more than transmit educational content: they have to cultivate students' ability to be creative, think critically, solve problems and make decisions; they have to help students work better together, by developing their ability to communicate and collaborate; they have to build students' capacity to recognise and exploit the potential of new technologies; and they have to nurture the character qualities that help people to live and work together.

Many, if not most, of the key attributes and skills of successful teachers will only become evident once teachers begin working in the classroom. Formal, measurable skills are necessary but not sufficient; they must be complemented by the intangible qualities that are difficult to quantify, including motivation and self-efficacy. And these qualities are often enhanced as teachers improve their performance and effectiveness through professional development activities – and as education systems recognise teachers' professionalism.

## TEACHERS AS PROFESSIONALS

The OECD Teaching and Learning International Survey (TALIS) built on international research to establish a conceptual framework for teacher professionalism. This framework describes teacher professionalism through teachers' knowledge base, autonomy and peer networks. As results from TALIS reveal, the meaning of teacher professionalism, and the nature and extent of professionalism practices, vary significantly across countries. In general, East Asian, Middle Eastern and Latin American systems grant less autonomy to teachers. This would suggest that the degree of decision making and control over school processes that teachers are accorded may be partly influenced by cultural norms. Meanwhile, only two of the education systems that emphasise peer networks are located in Europe, namely England (United Kingdom) and Romania.

To build teacher professionalism, policy makers and the profession itself must establish clearly and concisely what teachers are expected to know and be able to do. Teachers' work and the knowledge and skills that they need to be effective should reflect the learning objectives that schools aim to achieve. There needs to be profession-wide standards and a shared understanding of what counts as accomplished teaching. In general, teachers report that their formal education prepared them well for their work as teachers. On average, 93% of teachers reported being well or very well prepared to teach the content of their subjects, and 89% feel well or very well prepared in terms of the pedagogy and the practical components of the subjects they teach, even if, in some countries, this does not square with the levels of student achievement demonstrated in the comparative PISA surveys.

Given the rapid changes in education, the potentially long careers that many teachers have, and the need for updating skills, teachers' development must be viewed in terms of lifelong learning, with initial teacher education conceived as providing the foundation for ongoing learning, rather than producing ready-made professionals. Effective professional development activities forge a close connection between teachers' own development, their teaching responsibilities and their school's goals. The education policies that underpin these activities should aim to:

- prioritise the activities that have the greatest impact on teachers' practices
- include teachers in decision making at school
- strengthen peer collaboration through induction programmes and mentoring
- build a collaborative school culture
- support a culture of student assessment
- strengthen the links between teacher appraisal and professional development
- link professional autonomy with a collaborative culture

- involve teachers in developing professional standards
- strengthen teacher leadership
- engage teachers in education reform
- build teachers' capacity to use technology innovatively and effectively in the classroom.

## MOVING FROM POLICY TO PRACTICE

Implementing reform of any kind, in any sector, is never easy; but it is particularly difficult in the education sector. Assessing the relative costs and benefits of education reform is rendered particularly difficult by the large number of intervening variables that influence the nature, size and distribution of those benefits. It is rarely possible to predict clear, identifiable links between policies and outcomes, especially given the lag involved between the time at which the initial cost of reform is incurred, and the time when it is evident whether the intended benefits of reforms actually materialise.

As a result, there are a lot of stakeholders in education who have a vested interest in maintaining the status quo. Even small reforms can involve massive reallocations of resources, and touch the lives of millions on both the client and provider sides. This rules out "reform by stealth" and makes it essential to have consensus, or at least broad political support, for any proposed reform. In essence, education reform will not happen unless educators endorse and implement it.

Several policy lessons have emerged from OECD countries that have implemented reforms in education:

- Policy makers need to strive for consensus about the aims of education reform and engage stakeholders, especially teachers, in formulating and implementing policy responses, without compromising the drive for improvement.
- External pressures can be used to build a compelling case for change.
- All political players and stakeholders need to develop realistic expectations about the pace and nature of reforms to improve outcomes.
- Reforms need to be backed by sustainable financing.
- There is some shift away from reform initiatives per se towards building self-adjusting systems with feedback at all levels, incentives to react and tools to strengthen capacities to deliver better outcomes. Investment is needed in change-management skills. Teachers need reassurance that they will be given the tools to change and the recognition of their professional motivation to improve their students' outcomes.
- Evidence from international assessments, national surveys and inspectorates can be used to guide policy making. Evidence is most helpful when it is fed back to institutions along with information and tools about how they can use the information to improve outcomes.
- "Whole-of-government" approaches can include education in more comprehensive reforms. These need to be co-ordinated with all the relevant ministries.

Chapter 1

# WHAT KNOWLEDGE, SKILLS AND CHARACTER QUALITIES DO SUCCESSFUL TEACHERS REQUIRE?

The demands on student learning in the 21st century have profound implications for teachers and teaching. In addition to continuously updating their own knowledge of the subjects they teach, teachers are expected to work with multicultural classes, integrate students with special needs, be "assessment literate", work and plan in teams, assume some leadership roles and provide professional advice to parents, among other tasks. This chapter defines some of the knowledge, skills and character attributes required for effective teaching, including content and pedagogic knowledge, communication and organisational skills, and self-efficacy and motivation.

**Note regarding Israel**

The statistical data for Israel are supplied by and under the responsibility of the relevant Israeli authorities. The use of such data by the OECD is without prejudice to the status of the Golan Heights, East Jerusalem and Israeli settlements in the West Bank under the terms of international law.

The quality of education can never exceed the quality of teaching and teachers. But what exactly are the knowledge, skills and character qualities that will make teachers successful? How and to what extent are these related to teachers' education?

Some people explain poor learning outcomes in their country by claiming that their teachers come from the bottom third of their college graduates, while high-performing countries recruit their teachers from the top third. Surely, top school systems pay a great deal of attention to how they select their staff. They work hard to improve the performance of teachers who are struggling, they provide an environment in which teachers work together to frame good practice, and they establish intelligent pathways for teachers to grow in their careers. But does all that mean that in those countries the top third of graduates chose to become teachers rather than lawyers, doctors or engineers?

The Survey of Adult Skills, a product of the OECD Programme for the International Assessment of Adult Competencies (PIAAC), provides some insights into this issue. The survey tested the skills of countries' workforces – including teachers – in key areas such as numeracy, literacy and problem solving, making it possible to compare the numeracy and literacy skills of teachers with those of other college and university graduates (Figure 1.1). The results show that, among countries with comparable data, there is no country where teachers are in the top third of proficiency in these skills among all college-educated workers; and there is no country where they are among the bottom third of college graduates in these skills. In fact, teachers' skills in numeracy, literacy and problem solving tend to be similar to those of the average university-educated worker. There are just a few exceptions to this general trend: in Japan and Finland, for example, the average teacher has better numeracy skills than the average college graduate while in the Czech Republic, Denmark, Estonia, the Slovak Republic and Sweden, the reverse is true.

There is another way of looking at this. While, in each country, teachers tend to score similarly to college graduates on the numeracy test, the numeracy skills of the workforce as a whole differ substantially across countries. Consequently, the numeracy skills of teachers vary across countries too: teachers in Japan and Finland come out on top, followed by their Flemish (Belgium), German, Norwegian and Dutch counterparts. Teachers in Estonia, Italy, Poland and the United States come out at the bottom.

More sophisticated analyses show that there is, indeed, a relationship between the average numeracy skills of teachers in a given country and student performance in that country. But there are interesting exceptions to this pattern too. For example, teachers in one of the most rapidly improving education systems, Poland, scored low in numeracy, both in absolute and relative terms.

Together these results show that initial teacher qualifications are just one of many factors that influence the quality of learning. And unless countries have the luxury of hiring teachers from Finland or Japan, they need to think hard about making teaching a well-respected profession and a more attractive career choice – both intellectually and financially – and invest more in teacher development and competitive employment conditions. They can also learn from high-performing education systems how to transform the work organisation in their schools by replacing administrative forms of management with professional norms that provide the status and the high-quality training, responsibility and collaboration that go with professional work. They can develop effective systems of social dialogue, and appealing forms of employment that balance flexibility with job security, and that grant sufficient authority to schools to manage their talent.

But having discovered that teacher qualifications are only a rough proxy for the quality of teachers, at best, it is even more important to identify the knowledge, skills and character qualities that are common to the best teachers. The starting point for that exercise seems to be to look at what students need to know and be able to do in the years to come.

## WHAT STUDENTS NEED TO KNOW AND BE ABLE TO DO

The demands on learners, and thus on education systems, are evolving quickly. In the past, education was primarily about teaching people something; now, it's about making sure that students develop a reliable compass and the navigation skills to find their own way through an increasingly uncertain, volatile and ambiguous world. A generation ago, teachers could expect that what they taught would equip their students with the skills needed for the rest of their lives. Today, teachers need to prepare students for more rapid economic and social change than ever before, for jobs that have not yet been created, to use technologies that have not yet been invented, and to solve social problems that haven't arisen before. Undoubtedly, students – and teachers too – will make mistakes along the way. But it is often the mistakes and failures, once properly understood, that create the conditions for learning and growth.

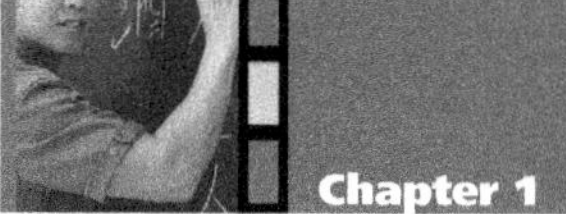


Figure 1.1

**Numeracy test scores of tertiary graduates and teachers**

*16-64 year-old tertiary graduates*

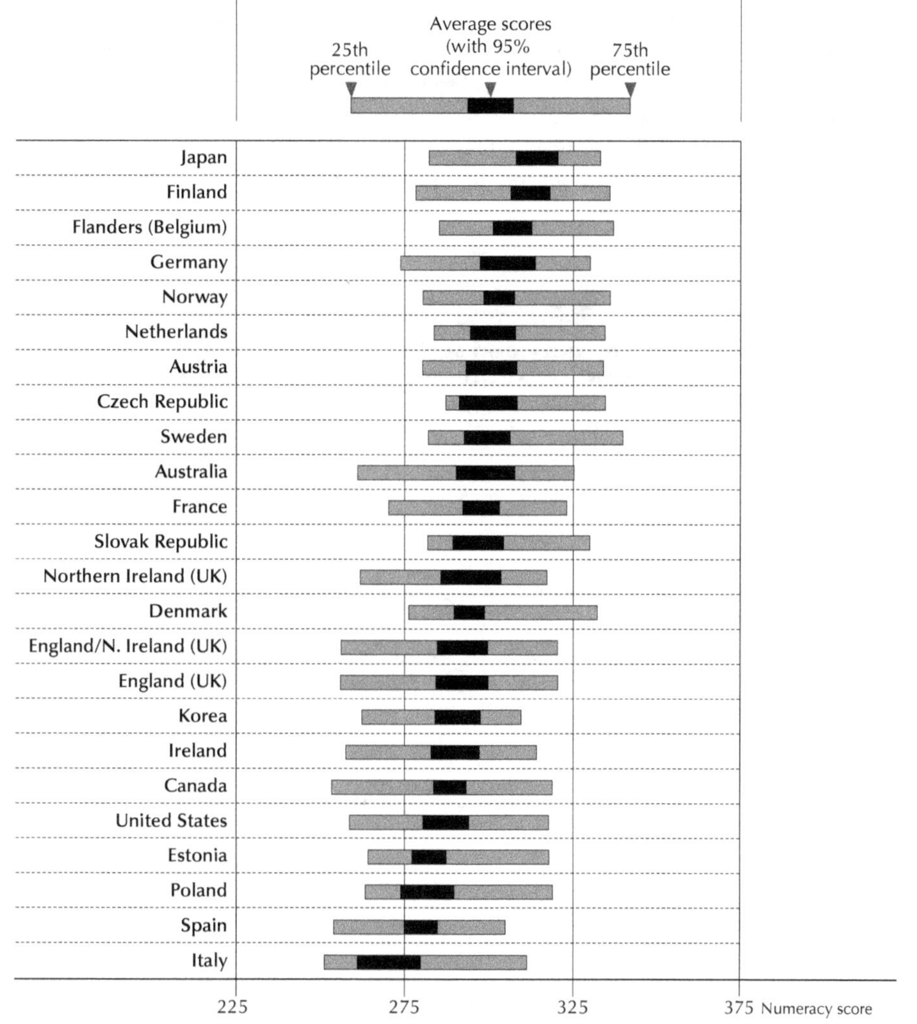


**Note:** The blue bar shows the middle half of the the distribution of numeracy skills of 16-64 year-old tertiary graduates (the end points are the 25th and 75th percentiles of the test scores) and the black segment shows the average numeracy scores of 16-64 year-old teachers (with a 95% confidence interval). *Countries are ranked in descending order of the average score.*

**Source:** Author's calculations based on the OECD Survey of Adult Skills (OECD, 2013).

StatLink http://dx.doi.org/10.1787/888933330323

How do we foster motivated, engaged learners who are prepared to conquer the unforeseen challenges of tomorrow, not to speak of those of today? The dilemma for teachers is that the kind of skills that are easiest to teach and easiest to test are also the skills that are easiest to digitise, automate and outsource. There is no question that state-of-the-art knowledge of specific disciplines will always remain the foundation of good teaching. Innovative and creative people generally have specialised skills in a field of knowledge or a practice. As much as "learning to learn" skills are important, we always learn by learning *something*. However, success in life and work is no longer mainly about reproducing content knowledge, but about extrapolating from what we know and applying that knowledge in novel situations.

Put simply, the world no longer rewards people just for what they know – Google knows more every day – but for what they can do with what they know. Because that is the main differentiator today, education has to do more than transmit educational content. It also has to cultivate students' ability to be creative, think critically, solve problems and make decisions. It has to help students work better together by developing their ability to communicate and collaborate. It has to build students' capacity to recognise and exploit the potential of new technologies. And, last but not least, it has to nurture the character qualities that help people to live and work together.

### Box 1.1 What learning strategies do students use most frequently?

An analysis of the Programme for International Student Assessment (PISA) results finds that it would be wrong to equate memorisation with poor learning outcomes and elaboration strategies, which involve making connections between tasks, prior knowledge and real-life experience, with improved learning. Indeed, results from PISA show that both memorisation and elaboration strategies can lead to better learning outcomes for students, even though the latter seems to be essential for solving more advanced tasks. That may be because students who use elaboration strategies also tend to report greater self-confidence in their mathematics ability, report less mathematics anxiety, are more open to problem solving, are more interested in mathematics, and are more likely to be perseverant in the face of difficulties (see Figures 1.a and 1.b).

Figure 1.a

**How students' mathematics anxiety and self-concept mediate the association between elaboration strategies and performance**

*Average across 45 education systems*

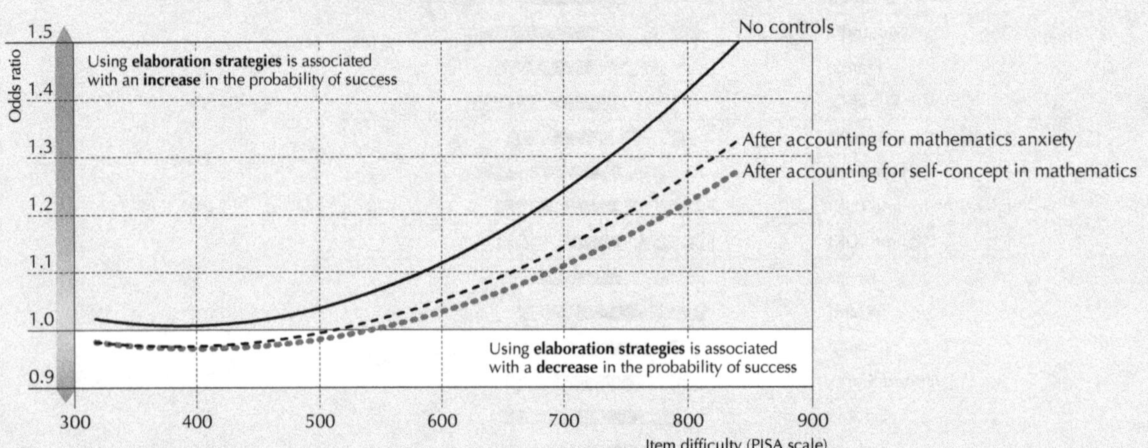


Source: OECD, PISA 2012 Database, http://pisa2012.acer.edu.au/.
StatLink http://dx.doi.org/10.1787/888933330332

Figure 1.b

**How students' attitudes mediate the association between elaboration strategies and mathematics performance**

*Average across 45 education systems*

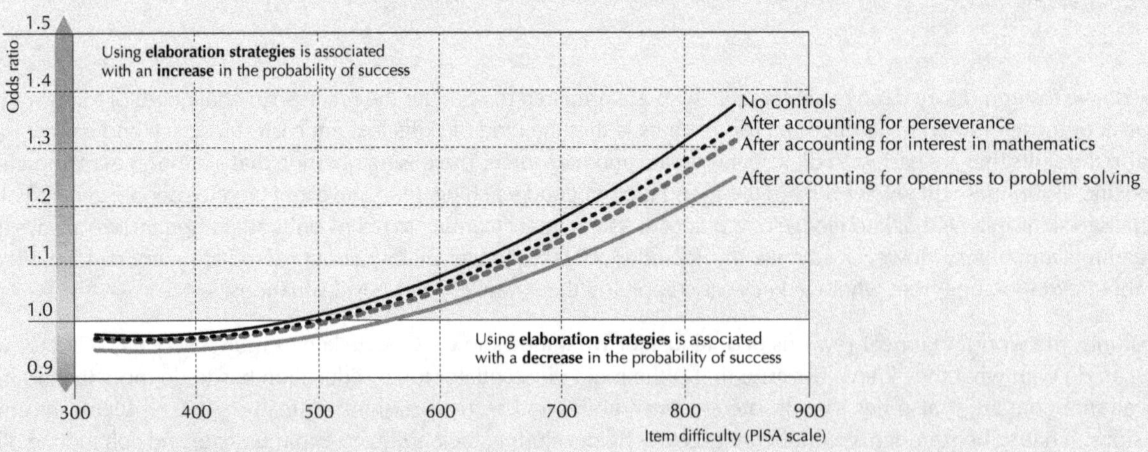


Source: OECD, PISA 2012 Database, http://pisa2012.acer.edu.au/.
StatLink http://dx.doi.org/10.1787/888933330349

...

It is an even greater mistake to equate teacher-centred approaches to learning, such as those that are prevalent in many East Asian countries, with memorisation or rote learning, while assuming that more student-centred approaches to teaching, such as having students work in small groups and/or independently, will automatically lead to better learning outcomes. As shown in Figures 1.c and 1.d, students in the English-speaking Western world appear to use memorisation strategies more than students in the East Asian education systems that participate in PISA use them. The reverse is true for students' use of elaboration strategies.

Figure 1.c

**Students' self-reported use of memorisation strategies**

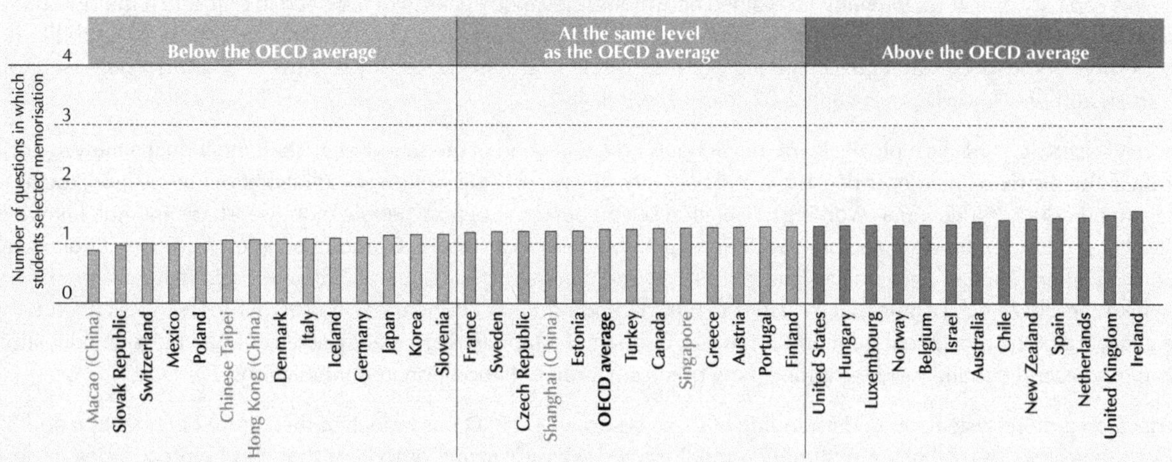


*Countries and economies are ranked in ascending order of the number of questions selected by students.*

**Source:** OECD, PISA 2012 Database, http://pisa2012.acer.edu.au/.

StatLink http://dx.doi.org/10.1787/888933330350

Figure 1.d

**Students' self-reported use of elaboration strategies**

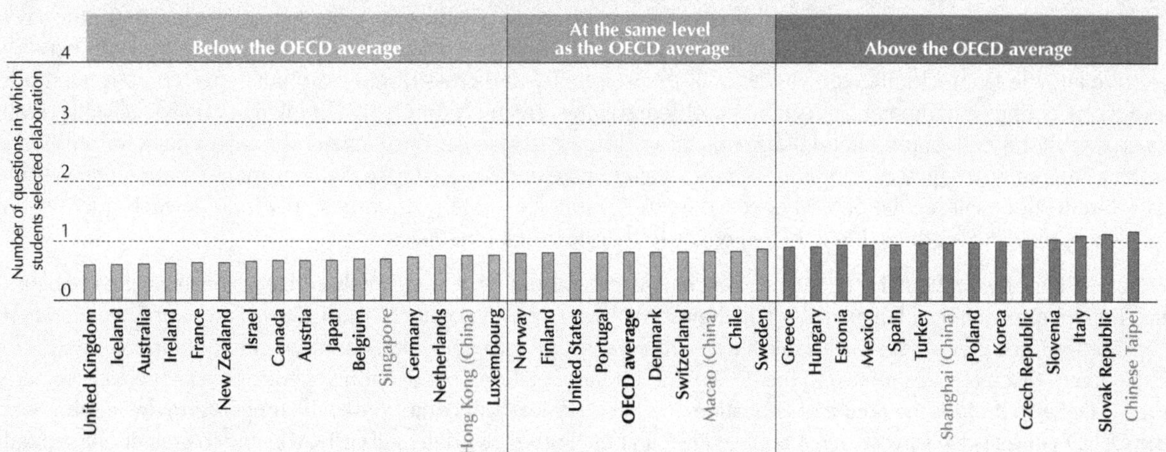


*Countries and economies are ranked in ascending order of the number of questions selected by students.*

**Source:** OECD, PISA 2012 Database, http://pisa2012.acer.edu.au/.

StatLink http://dx.doi.org/10.1787/888933330365

**Source:** Echazarra, A. and D. Salinas (forthcoming).

The world is no longer divided into specialists and generalists. Specialists generally have deep skills and narrow scope, giving them expertise that is recognised by peers, but not valued outside their domain. Generalists have broad scope but a shallow set of skills. What counts increasingly are the versatilists who are able to apply depth of skill to a progressively widening scope of situations and experiences. They acquire new competencies, build relationships, and assume new roles. They are capable of not only constantly adapting but of continuously learning and growing, of positioning themselves and repositioning themselves in a fast-changing world. They are also able to create value by making connections among ideas that previously seemed unrelated. This requires being familiar with and receptive to knowledge about fields other than the one chosen for intensive study. If people spend their whole lives in the silo of a single discipline, they will not be able to use their imaginations to connect the disparate dots and come up with the next invention.

Adaptability is the capacity to adjust to a changing environment. This trait was less important in the past, when established knowledge changed very little over a long period of time. Species that live in stable environments, for example, tend to lack this capacity. Today, adaptability has gained enormous relevance because of the need to adjust to a rapidly changing landscape (think of the species, including humans, that have to cope with climate change). Just as adaptability is the key to survival for species that face changing external conditions, it is the key for success in a world where technology advances and new knowledge is generated nearly every day.

In today's schools, students typically learn individually, and at the end of the school year, their individual achievements are certified. But the more interdependent the world becomes, the more society relies on collaboration. Innovation, too, is now rarely the product of individuals working in isolation but an outcome of how people mobilise, share and link knowledge. Schools need to prepare students for a world in which they will work and live among people of diverse cultural origins who hold different ideas, perspectives and values; a world where trust will have to bridge those differences; and a world in which their lives will be affected by issues that transcend national boundaries. In other words, schools need to be at the vanguard of the movement from education as a conduit of a rapidly depreciating stock of knowledge to education as a continuous and continuously expanding flow of information, collaboration and innovation.

To develop a more systematic understanding of these issues, the OECD has launched the Future of Education and Skills project that seeks to establish a multidimensional framework of learning outcomes that can help countries to design, develop and review their school systems. The dimensions covered by this framework will include knowledge and cognitive competencies and also broader outcomes, such as character, including social and emotional skills, and physical and mental well-being (Box 1.2).

### Box 1.2 The OECD Future of Education and Skills project

Those children who are beginning primary school today will start their professional careers in 2030, and those who are in secondary school today will become the core group of prime working-age adults in 2030. If today's students are to be able to seize new opportunities and meet foreseen or unforeseen challenges, they will need to acquire knowledge (including knowledge of both disciplinary and cross-disciplinary concepts, content, methods and tools), cognitive competencies (such as problem solving, creativity and critical thinking), and social skills (such as cross-cultural collaboration and communication). They will also need to develop broader character attributes (such as empathy, resilience, mindfulness, curiosity, courage and leadership) as well as meta-competencies (such as self-reflection, self-regulation and effective learning strategies). Many countries now include such qualities as resilience, respect for others, integrity and ethics in their learning objectives.

However, it is often difficult for countries to exchange ideas about what students should learn because the concepts, taxonomies and technical language used in their school systems vary so much. Through the Future of Education and Skills project, the OECD seeks to establish a common language through which countries can, both individually and collectively, discuss issues related to the design and implementation of education systems. Like its predecessor, the OECD DeSeCo project, the Future of Education and Skills project will contribute to the longer-term development of the OECD's large-scale surveys, most notably PISA and the Survey of Adult Skills (PIAAC), and to greater conceptual coherence among these surveys.

In addition to supporting studies on the types of knowledge, skills, values and character attributes that students will be expected to acquire in 2030, and how they influence learning and social outcomes later on, the project will include a survey of countries on curriculum design and implementation, and consultations among policy makers, experts/academics, employers and educators from around the world to validate the new OECD framework for the Future of Education and Skills.

### WHAT THIS MEANS FOR LEARNING ENVIRONMENTS AND THE ORGANISATION OF SCHOOLS

These demands on student learning have profound implications for teachers and teaching. The OECD has established core principles that underpin the learning environments and help to develop these kinds of knowledge and skills (OECD, 2015). These principles include making learning central; encouraging engagement; ensuring that learning is social and collaborative; and being sensitive to individual differences and to learners' motivations and attitudes. They also include being demanding of each learner without overload; using assessments to measure students' progress towards these goals, with emphasis on formative feedback; and promoting connections across learning activities and subjects, both in and outside of school.

But the status quo has many protectors. The 2008 OECD Teaching and Learning International Survey (TALIS) found that, across participating countries, an average of two in three teachers consider the school where they work to be essentially hostile to innovation. So it is no real surprise that changing learning environments is difficult.

It is therefore important to understand the design principles and conditions that can make innovation and modern learning environments systemic. This is about the interactions between the main players of innovative learning (learners, educators, content and learning resources) and the dynamics that connect those elements (pedagogy and formative evaluation, use of time, and the organisation of educators and learners). It also relates to the organisational features and leadership principles, recognising that learning environments and systems don't change by themselves but need strong design with vision and strategy. And it is about innovative partnerships, which are often neglected in education. This recognises that isolation within a world of complex learning systems seriously limits potential. In short, powerful learning environments will constantly be creating synergies and finding new ways to enhance professional, social and cultural capital with others. They will do this with families and communities, higher education, cultural institutions, businesses, and especially other schools and learning environments.

### WHAT THIS MEANS FOR TEACHERS

Society now expects teachers to deal effectively with students of different backgrounds and mother tongues, to be sensitive to culture and gender issues, to promote tolerance and social cohesion, to work with disadvantaged and immigrant students, and with students who have learning or behavioural problems, to use new technologies, and to keep pace with rapidly developing fields of knowledge and approaches to student assessment. Some of the challenges are emerging so quickly that it is not possible to anticipate them in initial teacher training programmes (Box 1.2).

Examples of the broader expectations for teachers include:

At the individual student level

- **Initiating and managing learning processes.** There is a lot of debate over how teachers should impart the curriculum, with rigor, focus and coherence of educational content at its core. But teachers are also expected to encourage students to take a more active role in their own learning. In a number of countries, providing stimulating settings for learning and helping students to develop problem-solving skills and to monitor and direct their own learning have become core responsibilities of teachers.
- **Responding to the learning needs of individual learners.** Teachers are expected to observe and diagnose students' strengths and weaknesses and to provide guidance, including on students' developmental needs, to individual learners and their parents.
- **Integrating formative and summative assessments.** Teachers need to be "assessment literate" with regard to both summative and formative methods. They need to be familiar with standardised assessment tests, to be able to use test results for diagnoses, and to be able to adapt curricula and teaching in response to student achievement.

At the classroom level

- **Teaching in multicultural classrooms.** As classes become more diverse, with students from different cultural and religious backgrounds, teachers are expected to foster social cohesion and integration by using appropriate classroom management techniques and applying cultural knowledge about different groups of students.
- **Emphasising cross-curricular studies.** Some school systems have introduced courses in such areas as citizenship education, covering community involvement, and social and moral responsibility, which are either taught separately or integrated across the school curriculum.

- **Integrating students with special needs.** School systems are increasingly offering integrated education for students with disabilities and learning difficulties, and teachers are expected to develop their knowledge of special education, appropriate teaching and management processes, and working with support personnel.

At the school level

- **Working and planning in teams.** Teachers are expected to collaborate and to work in teams with other teachers and staff members. They need social and management skills to co-operate, set common goals, and plan and monitor the attainment of goals set collaboratively.
- **Evaluating and planning for improvement.** In many systems, schools are now required to use data gathered from self-evaluation or through testing and external evaluations to inform school-development processes. This calls for new skills in data gathering and analysis, and in communicating the results to parents. In addition, school development requires project management and monitoring skills.
- **Using information and communication technologies (ICT) for teaching and administration.** Teachers are expected to integrate ICTs into their professional practice and to keep up to date with ICT developments and applications.
- **Projects between schools and international co-operation.** It is becoming more common for schools to collaborate on joint projects and to develop links with schools in other countries. These programmes require teachers with leadership and organisational skills, and the capacity to work and communicate effectively in a range of different settings.
- **Managing and sharing leadership.** In most countries, decision making in schools has become more decentralised in recent years, especially with regard to the organisation of instruction. An increase in the number and range of decisions taken at the school level has led to new managerial tasks for teachers; and in some countries teachers are expected to participate in and contribute to school leadership.

At the level of parents and the wider community

- **Providing professional advice to parents.** School systems increasingly emphasise the importance of close co-operation between schools and parents. Consequently, teachers need to be trained to know how and when to communicate with parents.
- **Building community partnerships for learning.** To gain additional support and offer broader learning experiences, schools in some countries are expected to build partnerships with community institutions and members, such as libraries, museums and employers. Teachers need to have the skills to make and maintain those connections.

This report discusses the knowledge, skills and character qualities that teachers need to acquire to fulfil these demands – and also the work organisation and the kind of support systems that are needed for them to do so.

## THE KNOWLEDGE, SKILLS AND CHARACTER ATTRIBUTES REQUIRED FOR EFFECTIVE TEACHING

### *Relationships between teaching and learning*

Much research has been devoted to exploring the impact of teachers and teaching on student achievement. This research shows that teacher quality is an important factor in determining gains in student achievement, even after accounting for prior student learning and family background characteristics.

Many comparative studies have found the **subject-specific knowledge** of teachers to be one of the main teacher-related determinants of improved learning outcomes. For example, while most international surveys of student performance do not find much of a relationship between the general level of education among teachers in an education system and student performance in that system, the share of teachers who have an advanced qualification in the subject they teach is often associated with better learning outcomes.

Using data from the Third International Mathematics and Science Study on 13-year-olds' achievement in 39 countries, Woessmann (2003) found that teachers' education in the subject they teach is positively related to student performance, with the effects stronger in science than in mathematics. The German COACTIV Study also shows how specific aspects of teacher competence are systematically related to differences in instructional quality (Baumert, 2011). A United States study by Goldhaber and Brewer (2000) found a positive relationship between teachers' higher-education degrees and student achievement in mathematics, but not in science.

The review by Wilson et al. (2001) found a positive connection between teachers' preparation in their subject matter and student performance, but also noted that more is not always better. They concluded that there is a threshold, measured in academic qualifications, of subject-matter knowledge necessary for effective teaching beyond which higher qualifications are not necessarily associated with student gains.

This conclusion supports that of Monk (1994), who found that teachers' preparation of content, as measured by coursework in the subject field, is positively related to student achievement in science, but that the relationship is curvilinear: beyond a certain level of coursework, student achievement diminishes. A review prepared for the Education Commission of the States concluded that research provides moderate support for the importance of subject-matter knowledge, but that it is generally "not fine-grained enough, however, to make it clear how much subject-matter knowledge is important for teaching specific courses and grade levels" (Education Commission of the States, 2003).

The evidence about the benefits of advanced qualifications in education is less clear. In the United States, for example, several states require that teachers earn a master's degree within a specific period of time after initial hiring. Most of these degrees are in education rather than in subject-matter content, and Rivkin et al. (2001) find no evidence that having a master's degree improves teachers' skills. In addition, such a policy raises the cost of choosing teaching as a career and may dissuade potentially effective teachers from entering the profession (Murnane, 1996). However, as a counter-example, all general education teachers in Finland are required to complete a five- to six-year course (a master's degree) before starting in the job. This is seen as contributing to teachers' relatively high social status and attracting competent people into the profession.

**Pedagogical knowledge** is important too. This knowledge of teaching and learning refers to the specialised body of knowledge concerned with creating effective teaching and learning environments for each and every student. It includes, for example, knowledge of how to structure learning objectives, how to plan a lesson, how to evaluate a lesson; knowledge of effective use of allocated time and strategies for differentiated instruction; and knowledge of how to design tasks for formative assessment. The knowledge also includes specialised areas of "learning", such as knowing how to facilitate learning given certain student characteristics, such as their prior knowledge, motivation and ability levels (Blömeke et al., 2008a; König et al., 2011; Shulman, 1986, 1987; Voss, Kunter and Baumert, 2011).

Studies looking at both subject-matter expertise and teaching methodology have shown that knowing how to teach also has positive effects on student achievement (Wenglinsky, 2000, 2002; Gustafsson, 2003; Wayne and Youngs, 2003). However, evaluating the impact of pedagogical preparation is made difficult because there is such a wide range of courses under this label, including courses in subject-specific teaching and more generic courses in learning theory, educational psychology, sociology, assessment, measurement and testing, classroom management, and so on. These courses are offered in different sequences and with differing content and intensity. Rice (2003) concludes that pedagogical coursework contributes to teacher effectiveness when combined with content knowledge. According to some, the United States research supports the conclusion that pedagogical preparation contributes to effective teaching, especially subject-specific courses and those designed to develop core skills, such as classroom management, student assessment and curriculum development (Education Commission of the States, 2003).

Results from PISA 2012 (Echazarra and Salinas, forthcoming) provide some interesting insights into the prevalence of different pedagogical strategies (Figure 1.2) and their relationships with learning outcomes (Figures 1.3 and 1.4). According to students' reports, the "traditional" teacher-directed methods of instruction were among the most frequently used. On average across OECD countries, eight out of ten students (80%) reported having a mathematics teacher who tells them what they have to learn. Similarly, about seven out of ten OECD students reported having a mathematics teacher who asks questions to check whether students understood the material (71%) or who set clear goals for student learning (69%).

Cognitive-activation strategies were also frequently used, particularly those in which teachers ask students to explain how they solved a problem. On average across OECD countries, 70% of students reported that their teachers ask them to do this. More than one in two students across OECD countries also reported that their teachers use other cognitive-activation strategies, such as asking students to explain how they solved a problem, asking students to apply what they have learned to new contexts, helping students to learn from mistakes, giving students problems that can be solved in several different ways, asking questions that make students reflect on how to solve a problem, presenting problems in different contexts so that students know whether they have understood the concepts, and giving students problems that require them to think for an extended time.

In contrast, student-oriented instructional practices, such as having students work in small groups, conducting projects that require at least one week to complete, or asking students to help plan classroom activities, were the least frequently used, on average across countries. The most common of these strategies was giving different work to students based on the speed with which they learned. Fewer than one in three students in OECD countries reported that their teachers did this. Formative-assessment techniques were also infrequently used in mathematics classes, with the exception of telling students what is expected of them for tests, quizzes and assignments. Around 60% of students reported that their teachers did this.

Figure 1.2

**Teaching strategies in OECD countries**

*Percentage of students who responded that in every or most mathematics lessons:*

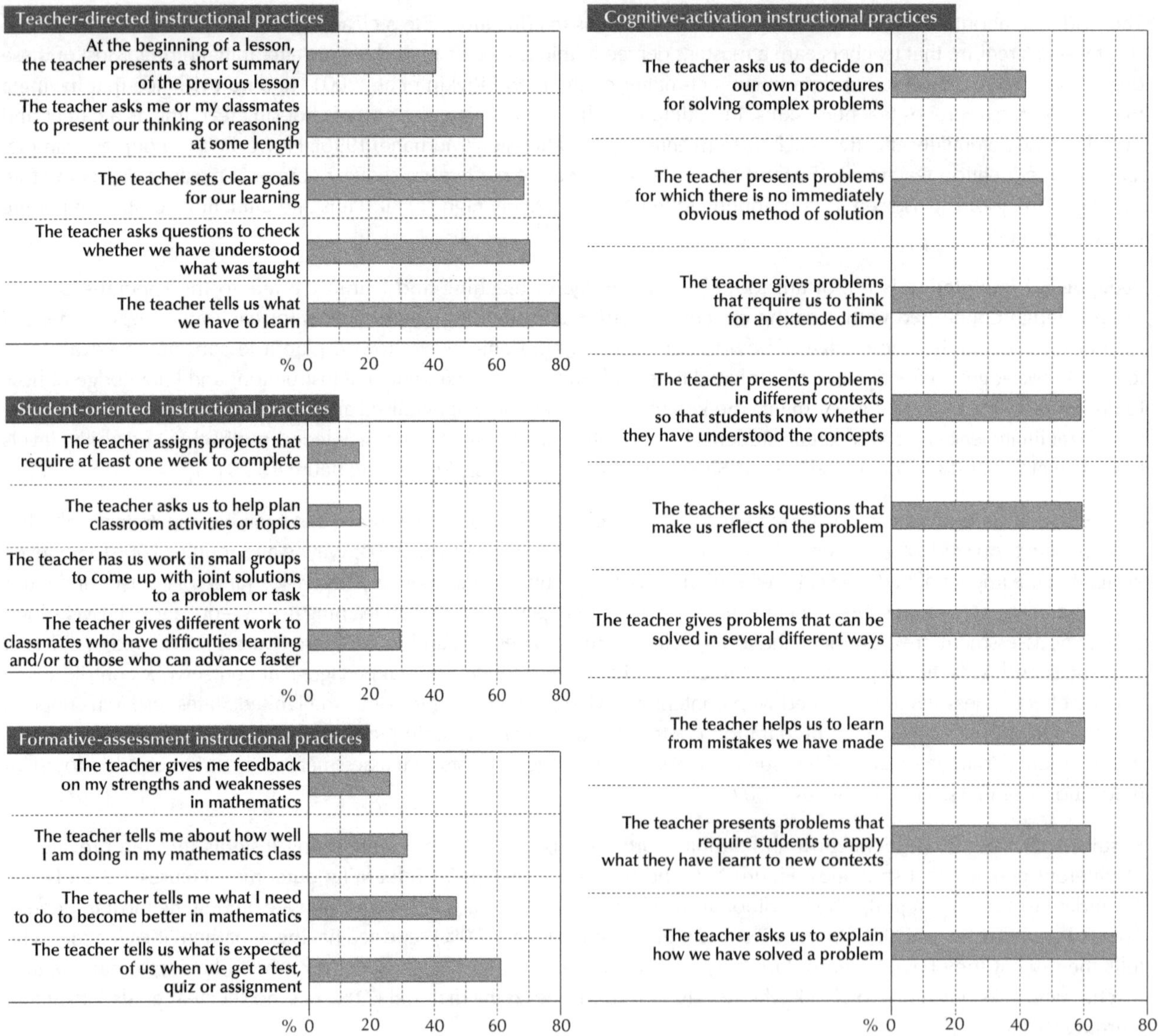

**Source:** OECD, PISA 2012 Database, Tables 3.1, 3.2, 3.3 and 3.4, http://pisa2012.acer.edu.au/.

*StatLink* http://dx.doi.org/10.1787/888933330377

Results from PISA show that, on average across OECD countries, students who scored at the lower levels of mathematics proficiency, particularly at or below Level 1, most frequently reported that they are exposed to student-oriented, formative-assessment and teacher-directed instruction. Conversely, students who reported greater exposure to cognitive-activation instruction scored, on average, at higher levels of proficiency in mathematics, notably at Level 5 or 6 (Figure 1.5).

Figure 1.3

## Differences across countries in teacher-directed instruction

**Percentage of students who reported that their mathematics teacher (in every/most lessons):**

- A Tells students what they have to learn
- B Presents a short summary of previous lesson
- C Sets clear goals for students' learning
- D Asks them or their classmates to present their thinking or reasoning at some length
- E Asks questions to check whether they have understood what was taught

| | A | B | C | D | E |
|---|---|---|---|---|---|
| Shanghai (China) | 86 | 70 | 78 | 70 | 77 |
| Greece | 81 | 45 | 76 | 61 | 78 |
| Korea | 76 | 48 | 60 | 30 | 59 |
| Turkey | 79 | 56 | 69 | 77 | 76 |
| Slovenia | 81 | 50 | 71 | 64 | 68 |
| Japan | 74 | 40 | 58 | 48 | 63 |
| Hungary | 85 | 44 | 61 | 55 | 72 |
| France | 79 | 49 | 61 | 53 | 65 |
| Czech Republic | 78 | 54 | 74 | 60 | 75 |
| Macao (China) | 73 | 57 | 65 | 45 | 67 |
| Chile | 84 | 54 | 82 | 53 | 82 |
| Ireland | 84 | 29 | 59 | 57 | 75 |
| Belgium | 83 | 42 | 61 | 47 | 68 |
| Luxembourg | 85 | 34 | 57 | 59 | 63 |
| Mexico | 73 | 54 | 82 | 61 | 79 |
| Chinese Taipei | 74 | 46 | 63 | 49 | 70 |
| Austria | 80 | 40 | 65 | 60 | 64 |
| Israel | 87 | 41 | 74 | 68 | 72 |
| Netherlands | 77 | 30 | 67 | 72 | 60 |
| **OECD average** | 80 | 41 | 69 | 56 | 71 |
| Germany | 80 | 34 | 67 | 68 | 70 |
| Canada | 82 | 56 | 71 | 59 | 76 |
| Singapore | 88 | 50 | 71 | 59 | 82 |
| Finland | 78 | 44 | 67 | 62 | 60 |
| United States | 83 | 49 | 74 | 65 | 80 |
| Portugal | 80 | 47 | 78 | 75 | 78 |
| Australia | 85 | 41 | 68 | 56 | 73 |
| Slovak Republic | 79 | 45 | 74 | 44 | 70 |
| Estonia | 88 | 28 | 75 | 36 | 68 |
| Hong Kong (China) | 69 | 43 | 49 | 43 | 63 |
| Iceland | 89 | 31 | 80 | 39 | 71 |
| United Kingdom | 87 | 39 | 75 | 57 | 80 |
| Switzerland | 76 | 39 | 70 | 67 | 68 |
| Spain | 66 | 38 | 73 | 46 | 72 |
| Sweden | 77 | 34 | 67 | 71 | 68 |
| Italy | 75 | 35 | 68 | 47 | 71 |
| Poland | 81 | 27 | 69 | 43 | 66 |
| New Zealand | 84 | 40 | 57 | 54 | 69 |
| Norway | 76 | 27 | 64 | 61 | 64 |
| Denmark | 75 | 30 | 67 | 31 | 76 |

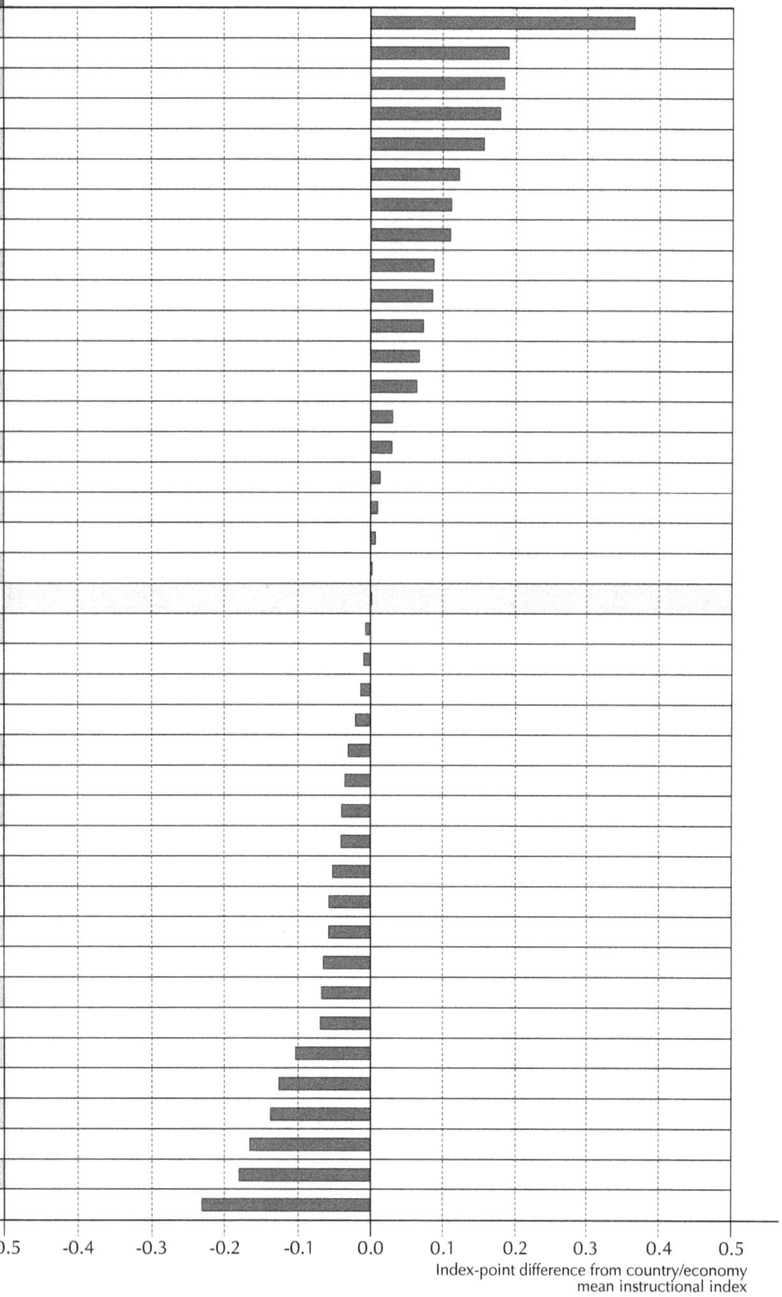

-0.5 -0.4 -0.3 -0.2 -0.1 0.0 0.1 0.2 0.3 0.4 0.5

Index-point difference from country/economy mean instructional index

**Note:** For each country/economy, the index of teacher-directed instruction was substracted from the mean of the four PISA instructional indices.

*Countries and economies are ranked in descending order of the index-point difference (average of the four PISA indices minus the index of teacher-directed instruction).*

**Source:** OECD, PISA 2012 Database, Tables 3.1 and 3.5, http://pisa2012.acer.edu.au/.

StatLink http://dx.doi.org/10.1787/888933330388

Figure 1.4

## Differences across countries in student-oriented instruction

**Percentage of students who declare that their mathematics teacher (in every/most lessons):**

- A Has them work in small groups
- B Gives different work to students who have difficulties learning and/or to those who can advance faster
- C Assigns projects that require at least one week to complete
- D Asks them to help plan classroom activities or topics

| | A | B | C | D |
|---|---|---|---|---|
| Sweden | 33 | 62 | 19 | 13 |
| Korea | 14 | 16 | 11 | 21 |
| Iceland | 22 | 47 | 30 | 11 |
| Norway | 21 | 58 | 11 | 11 |
| Macao (China) | 22 | 26 | 20 | 12 |
| Japan | 14 | 32 | 13 | 15 |
| Denmark | 30 | 29 | 13 | 12 |
| Mexico | 52 | 30 | 29 | 27 |
| Switzerland | 37 | 34 | 19 | 18 |
| Turkey | 25 | 37 | 23 | 27 |
| Chinese Taipei | 16 | 22 | 17 | 23 |
| Chile | 42 | 26 | 31 | 21 |
| Slovak Republic | 16 | 33 | 15 | 26 |
| Netherlands | 23 | 25 | 17 | 18 |
| Finland | 11 | 56 | 6 | 5 |
| Italy | 15 | 13 | 10 | 46 |
| Czech Republic | 13 | 26 | 8 | 37 |
| **OECD average** | 23 | 30 | 17 | 17 |
| Israel | 20 | 39 | 28 | 19 |
| Germany | 27 | 25 | 12 | 14 |
| Poland | 19 | 28 | 13 | 10 |
| United States | 50 | 19 | 30 | 17 |
| Estonia | 9 | 33 | 6 | 11 |
| New Zealand | 24 | 37 | 20 | 13 |
| Portugal | 36 | 37 | 22 | 26 |
| Spain | 17 | 22 | 17 | 18 |
| Luxembourg | 19 | 24 | 14 | 16 |
| Hong Kong (China) | 15 | 15 | 11 | 11 |
| Belgium | 14 | 21 | 12 | 16 |
| Australia | 17 | 27 | 23 | 11 |
| Singapore | 26 | 28 | 17 | 18 |
| Canada | 37 | 22 | 17 | 13 |
| Austria | 21 | 21 | 11 | 14 |
| Greece | 18 | 16 | 16 | 26 |
| United Kingdom | 20 | 34 | 21 | 8 |
| Slovenia | 14 | 25 | 15 | 17 |
| France | 16 | 13 | 13 | 9 |
| Hungary | 12 | 22 | 8 | 9 |
| Shanghai (China) | 24 | 18 | 10 | 15 |
| Ireland | 12 | 16 | 7 | 6 |



**Note:** For each country/economy, the *index of student-oriented instruction* was substracted from the mean of the four PISA instructional indices.
*Countries and economies are ranked in descending order of the index-point difference (average of the four PISA indices minus the* index of student-oriented instruction*).*

**Source:** OECD, PISA 2012 Database, Tables 3.2 and 3.5, http://pisa2012.acer.edu.au/.

StatLink http://dx.doi.org/10.1787/888933330398

Figure 1.5

**Teaching strategies, by students' proficiency in mathematics**

*OECD average*

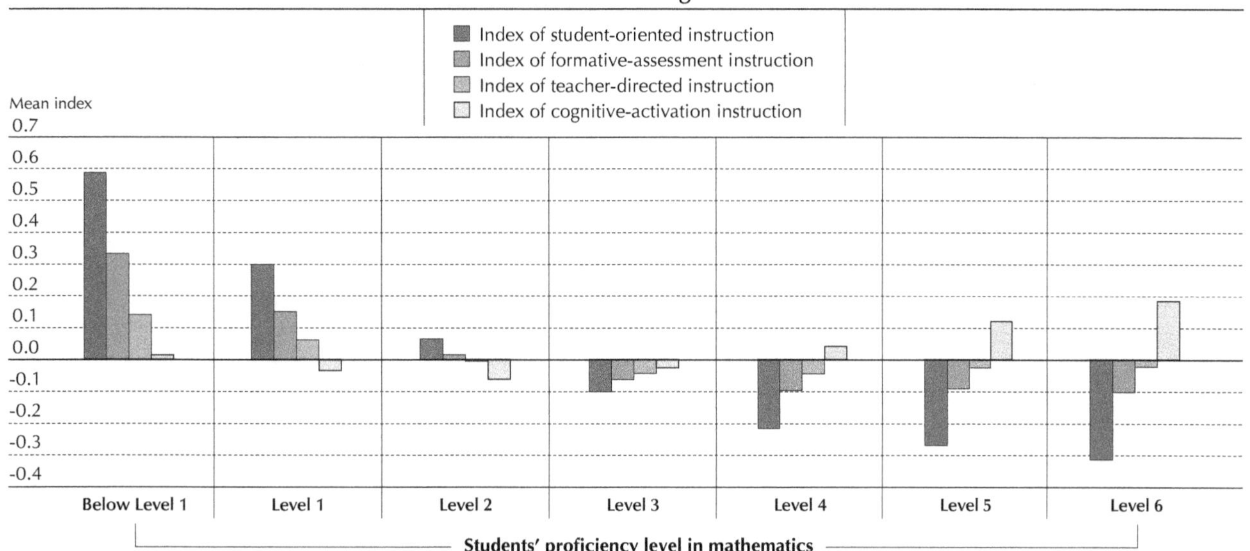


**Source:** OECD, PISA 2012 Database, Table 3.24, http://pisa2012.acer.edu.au/.
StatLink http://dx.doi.org/10.1787/888933330406

Figures 1.6 through 1.9 show the relationship between each instructional strategy and students' mean mathematics score in PISA, before and after accounting for the other three instructional strategies considered in this analysis. These figures reveal that cognitive-activation instruction has the greatest positive association with students' mean mathematics score, on average across OECD countries. Before accounting for other teaching strategies, cognitive-activation instruction is associated with an increase of about five score points on the PISA mathematics assessment. After accounting for the other three teaching strategies, the average improvement in mathematics performance associated with cognitive-activation instruction is as large as 19 score points. Remarkably, after accounting for the other teaching strategies, there is a positive association between cognitive-activation instruction and mean mathematics performance in every country and economy that participated in PISA 2012, except Albania.

Results from PISA also show that these teaching strategies are associated with the learning environment and organisation of schools. For example, schools in which these teaching strategies are used more frequently tend to be those with more supportive teachers, where there are good teacher-student relations, where teachers are skilled in managing their classrooms and maintain discipline, and are those whose students reported feeling a greater sense of belonging at school.

The strength of the relationship between the learning environment and instructional strategies is greater with teacher-directed and cognitive-activation strategies, and is weaker with student-oriented strategies. Student-oriented instruction is something of an exception in that its relationship with classroom discipline is weak and often negative, most likely because small-group discussions or other methods that aim to give students a more active role in the learning process can generate or require a more dynamic – and, to some, louder – classroom environment.

Of course, the pedagogical knowledge base is not static: **new knowledge** emerges from research or is shared through professional communities. As professionals, teachers are expected to process and evaluate new knowledge relevant to their core professional practice and regularly update their profession's knowledge base.

New knowledge also emerges from the interdisciplinary field known as the "science of learning", which includes the field of educational neurosciences. This latter field has made considerable progress in understanding how the human brain processes, encodes and retrieves information. Understanding how the brain works can inform teachers' pedagogical practice. It can, for example, help them to design and structure lessons that enable "deep learning" (rather than surface learning) and to adapt lessons based on individual students' prior knowledge, motivation and ability levels. In this respect, those who teach the teachers can be expected to have more current knowledge, and the capacity to transform research knowledge into practical knowledge. That is how findings from learning research can best be incorporated into the profession.

Figure 1.6

**Mathematics performance and cognitive-activation instruction**

*Score-point difference in mathematics associated with one-unit increase in the* index of cognitive-activation instruction

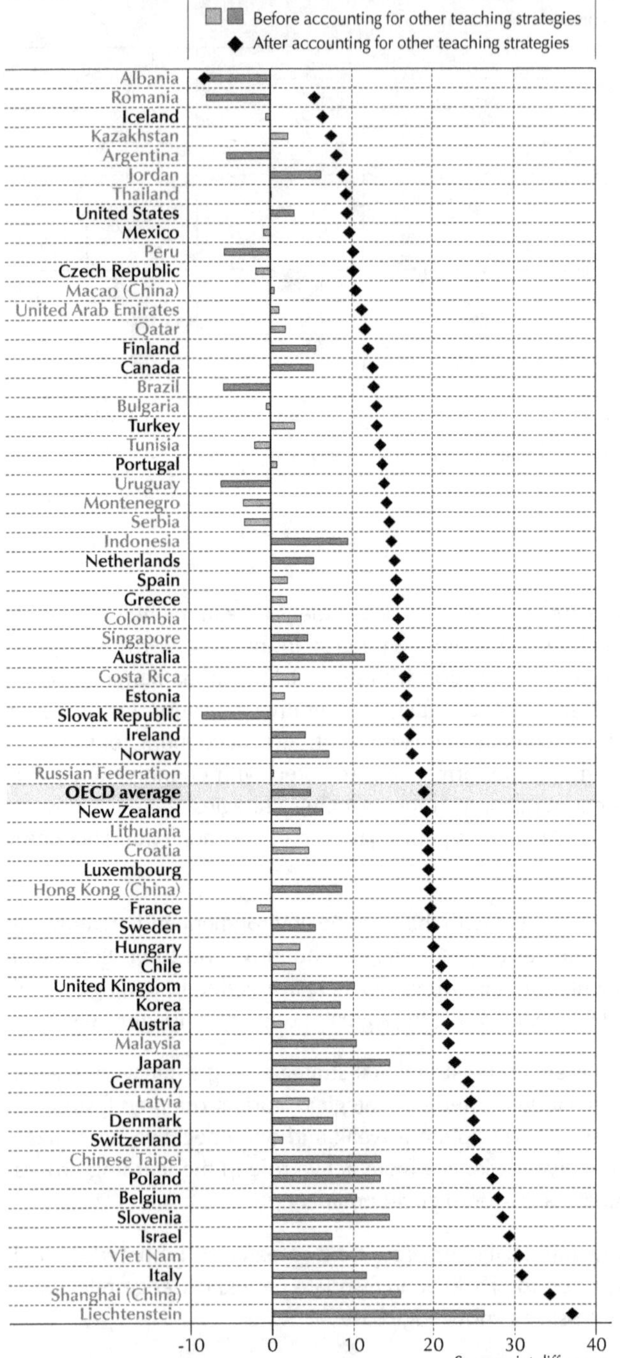


**Notes:** Score-point difference in mathematics that is statistically significant is marked in a darker tone.

"Other teaching strategies" refers to the PISA indices of teacher-directed, student-oriented and formative-assessment instruction.

*Countries and economies are ranked in ascending order of the score-point difference in mathematics, after accounting for other teaching strategies.*

**Source:** OECD, PISA 2012 Database, Tables 3.25, http://pisa2012.acer.edu.au/.

StatLink http://dx.doi.org/10.1787/888933330414

Figure 1.7

**Mathematics performance and student-oriented instruction**

*Score-point difference in mathematics associated with one-unit increase in the* index of student-oriented instruction

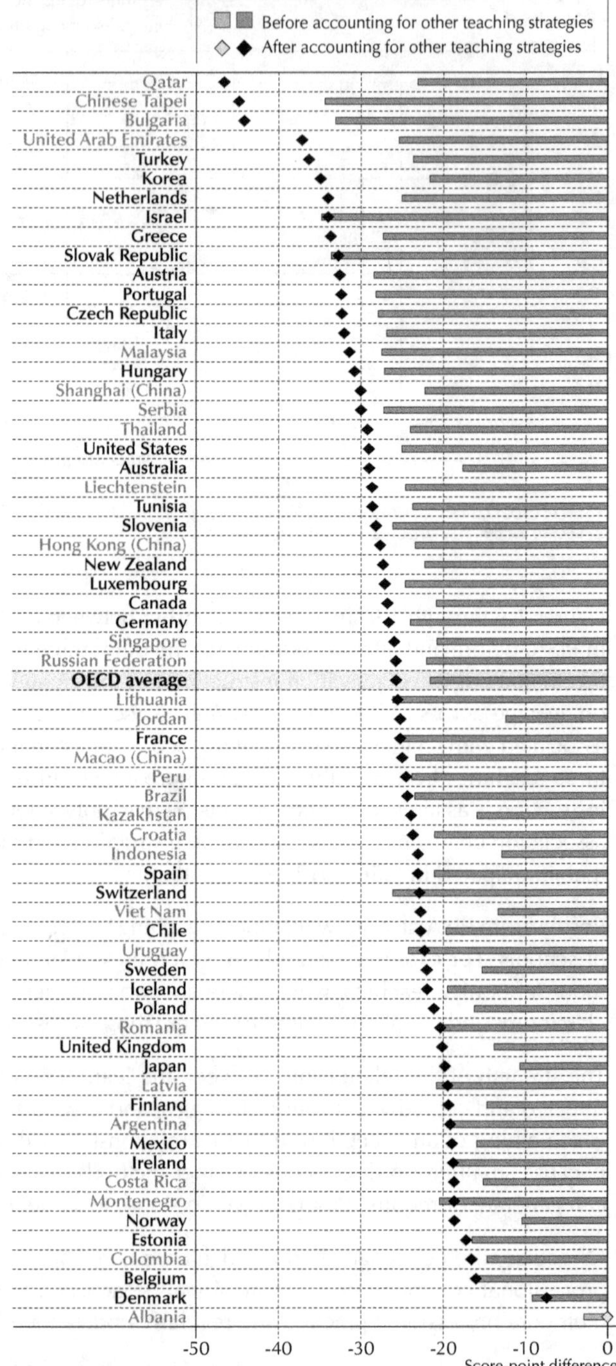


**Notes:** Score-point difference in mathematics that is statistically significant is marked in a darker tone.

"Other teaching strategies" refers to the PISA indices of teacher-directed, cognitive-activation and formative-assessment instruction.

*Countries and economies are ranked in ascending order of the score-point difference in mathematics, after accounting for other teaching strategies.*

**Source:** OECD, PISA 2012 Database, Tables 3.25, http://pisa2012.acer.edu.au/.

StatLink http://dx.doi.org/10.1787/888933330424

Figure 1.8

### Mathematics performance and formative-assessment instruction

*Score-point difference in mathematics associated with one-unit increase in the* index of formative-assessment instruction

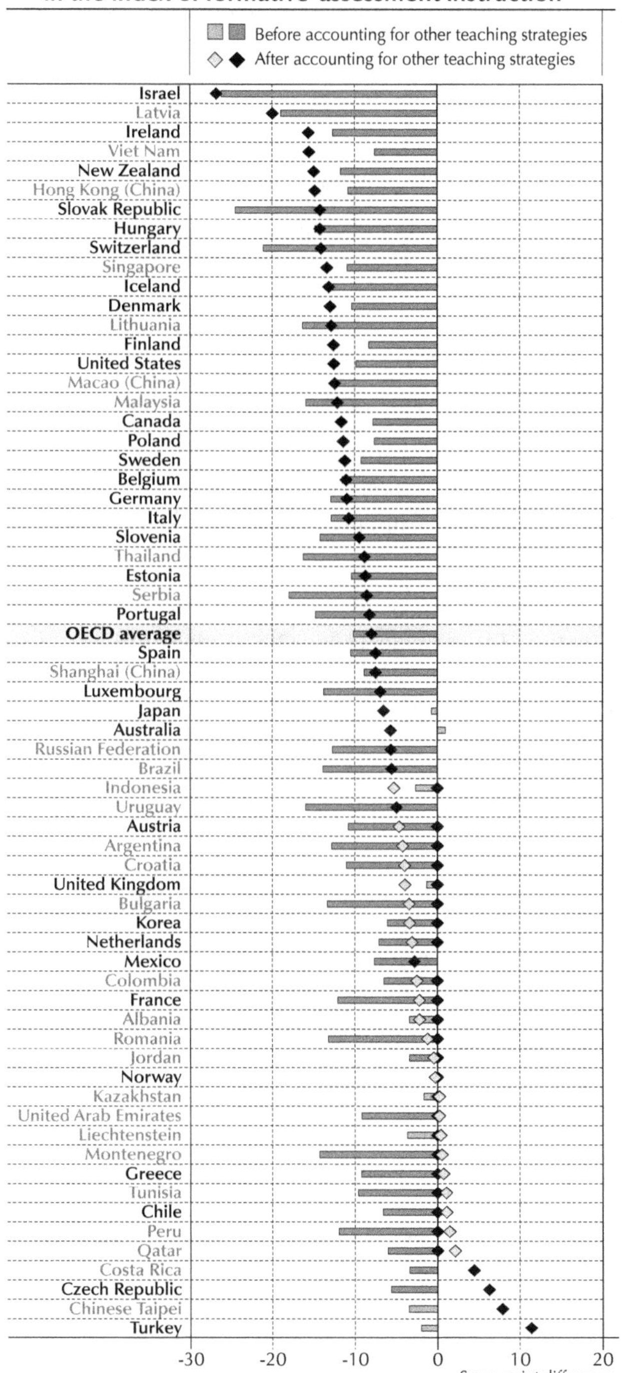


**Notes:** Score-point difference in mathematics that is statistically significant is marked in a darker tone.

"Other teaching strategies" refers to the PISA indices of teacher-directed, student-oriented and cognitive-activation instruction.

*Countries and economies are ranked in ascending order of the score-point difference in mathematics, after accounting for other teaching strategies.*

**Source:** OECD, PISA 2012 Database, Tables 3.25, http://pisa2012.acer.edu.au/.

StatLink http://dx.doi.org/10.1787/888933330436

Figure 1.9

### Mathematics performance and teacher-directed instruction

*Score-point difference in mathematics associated with one-unit increase in the* index of teacher-directed instruction

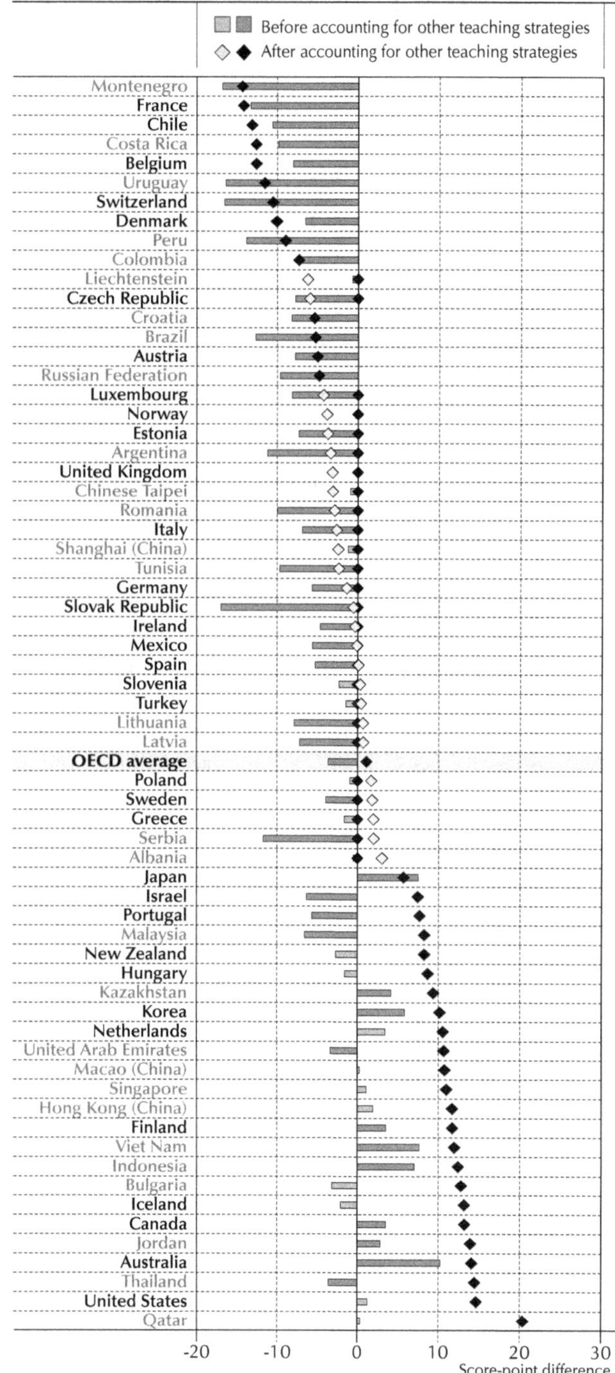


**Notes:** Score-point difference in mathematics that is statistically significant is marked in a darker tone.

"Other teaching strategies" refers to the PISA indices of cognitive-activation, student-oriented and formative-assessment instruction.

*Countries and economies are ranked in ascending order of the score-point difference in mathematics, after accounting for other teaching strategies.*

**Source:** OECD, PISA 2012 Database, Tables 3.25, http://pisa2012.acer.edu.au/.

StatLink http://dx.doi.org/10.1787/888933330448

### *Some attributes of effective teachers*

Teaching is a complex task that involves interactions with a great variety of learners in a wide range of different circumstances. It is clear there is not a single set of teacher attributes and behaviours that is universally effective for all types of students and learning environments, especially when schooling varies in many ways across different countries. That said, one consistent finding is that effective teachers are intellectually capable people who are articulate and knowledgeable, and are able to think, communicate and plan systematically. Students achieve more with teachers who perform well on tests of literacy and verbal ability (Gustafsson, 2003; Rice, 2003).

In an influential study, Shulman (1992) identified five broad areas for the development of professional knowledge and expertise in teaching:

**Behaviour** – effectiveness is evidenced by teacher behaviour and student learning outcomes.

**Cognition** – teachers as intelligent, thoughtful, sentient beings, characterised by intentions, strategies, decisions and reflections.

**Content** – the nature and adequacy of teacher knowledge of the substance of the curriculum being taught.

**Character** – the teachers serve as moral agents, deploying a moral-pedagogical craft.

**Knowledge** of, and sensitivity to, the cultural, social and political contexts and the environments of their students.

Studies by Lingard et al. (2002) and Ayres et al. (2000) identified a range of personal competencies that influence the quality and effectiveness of teaching: sound subject knowledge; communication skills; the ability to relate to individual students; self-management skills; organisational skills; classroom-management skills; problem-solving skills; a repertoire of teaching methods; teamwork skills; and research skills.

A key question for research and policy has always been: What distinguishes excellent teaching from merely good teaching? One strand of research tries to identify the attributes of expert teachers. For example, Hattie (2003) drew on an extensive review of research to identify five essential skills that distinguish highly competent teachers. He considers expert teachers as those who can: identify essential representations of their subject, based on how they organise and use their content knowledge; guide learning through classroom interactions by creating optimal classroom environments; monitor student learning and provide feedback; promote effective outcomes through the manner in which they treat students, and their passion for teaching and learning; and influence student outcomes by engaging students, providing challenging tasks and goals, and enhancing "deep" learning or understanding.

Based on a review of the literature reported in Berliner (2001, 2004), expert teachers are characterised as those who: make better use of knowledge; have extensive knowledge of pedagogical content, including deep representations of subject-matter knowledge; have better problem-solving strategies; can better adapt and modify goals to suit individual diverse learners; can improvise better; are better at making decisions; present more challenging objectives; maintain better classroom climate; have better perceptions of classroom events; are better able to read cues from students; are more sensitive to context; monitor learning better and provide feedback to students; test hypotheses more frequently; hold greater respect for students; and display more passion for teaching.

Sternberg and Horvath (1995) used findings from psychological research to distinguish experts from novices. They found that experts bring more knowledge to bear in solving problems than do novices; experts are able to solve problems more efficiently than are novices; and experts are more able to arrive at insightful solutions to problems than are novices. According to Sternberg and Horvath, it is the store of knowledge that expert teachers hold that accounts for their ability to solve problems more efficiently and to arrive at more insightful solutions than novices.

Westerman (1991) investigated how teachers develop their decision-making skills and found that one of the notable differences between novices and experts was the latter's ability to combine new subject-content knowledge with prior knowledge.

Many, if not most, of the key attributes and skills of successful teachers will only become evident once they are in the job. Formal, measurable skills are necessary but not sufficient; they must be complemented by the intangible qualities that are difficult to quantify. Processes must be put in place to identify those qualities when determining who enters teacher education, the criteria for qualification as a teacher, and the basis on which teachers are selected for employment and career advancement.

### *Beyond knowledge and skills*

Based on a review of various professions, including the medical profession, Kunter et al. (2013) suggest that "competence" can be defined as the "skills, knowledge, attitudes, and motivational variables that form the basis for mastery of specific situations" and that these characteristics are both learnable and teachable. "Professional competence" is demonstrated when mastery of situations is dependent on the application of knowledge, skills, attitudes and motivation to highly complex and demanding professions, such as teaching. It follows from this conceptualisation of professional competence that the ability to solve work-related problems requires having not only the cognitive abilities for developing effective solutions (i.e. pedagogical knowledge), but also the right motivation and attitudes (Blömeke and Delaney, 2012).

Several studies reviewed by the OECD indicate that motivation is strongly related to high-quality instruction and is positively related to student achievement and non-cognitive outcomes. Positive associations are observed between teacher motivation and teacher-reported or student-reported use of instructional practices that emphasise student learning, mastery-oriented instruction, co-operative learning and student differentiation (e.g. Ciani, Summers and Easter, 2008; Lauermann, 2015; Thoonen et al., 2011).

A positive relationship is found between teacher motivation and teacher-reported or student-reported use of cognitive-activation teaching strategies, classroom management, individual learning support by the teacher, and positive teacher-student relationships (e.g. Butler, 2012; Butler and Shibaz, 2014; Holzberger, Philipp and Kunter, 2013, 2014; Kunter and Baumert, 2006; Kunter et al., 2008). Caprara, Barbaranelli, Steca and Malone (2006) also reported a positive relationship between teachers' motivation and student achievement even after controlling for prior achievement. Thoonen, Sleegers, Peetsma and Oort (2011) reported a positive association between teacher motivation and student-reported well-being at school.

Kunter et al. (2013) reported a positive relationship between student achievement and motivation on the one hand and better instructional quality on the other because these teachers provided more cognitive-activation instruction and better learning support and classroom management.

Other researchers (Blömeke and Delaney, 2012; Blömeke et al., 2008), who are conducting empirical investigations of teachers' professional competence, propose a model in which professional competence comprises cognitive abilities (i.e. professional knowledge, such as content knowledge, pedagogical-content knowledge and general pedagogical knowledge) and affective-motivational characteristics (defined as professional beliefs about teaching, learning and the subject content, motivation and self-regulation).

Empirical investigations of teachers' professional competence are in their early stages. The few studies conducted thus far indicate that pedagogical knowledge is a critical component of teaching competence, but that knowledge alone is insufficient. Psychological factors, such as beliefs, motivation and self-regulation, are also part of teaching competence.

## TEACHERS' OWN PERSPECTIVE ON PROFESSIONAL COMPETENCY

An important aspect of any profession is the development of what the psychologist Albert Bandura (1995) has called self-efficacy. Self-efficacy is the belief in one's ability to accomplish tasks in particular circumstances. Self-efficacy in teaching is a teacher's belief that he or she can have a positive impact on pupils, even in adverse conditions and circumstances. So it is helpful to look at issues surrounding professional competency from the teachers' perspective. In the majority of countries participating in the 2013 TALIS survey, most teachers reported holding beliefs that suggest high levels of self-efficacy. On average across countries, between 80% and 92% of teachers reported that they can often get students to believe they can do well in school, help students to value learning, craft good questions for students, control disruptive behaviour in the classroom, articulate their expectations about student behaviour, help students to think critically, get students to follow classroom rules, calm a disruptive student, use a variety of assessment strategies, and provide alternative explanations when students are confused.

However, when teachers' perceptions of self-efficacy in these domains are compared to student learning outcomes (as measured by the OECD Programme for International Student Assessment [PISA]), those perceptions appear to be overly optimistic. In comparison, far fewer teachers reported that they are highly confident in their ability to motivate students who show low interest in school work (70%) and can use alternative instructional strategies (77%).

Yet in some countries, compared with the overall average, teachers seem to believe less – significantly and consistently – in their ability to have a positive influence in these domains. Notably, teachers in the Czech Republic and Japan reported lower levels of confidence in their abilities in some areas.

Does it make a difference? In a recent study of factors determining teacher quality and effectiveness, Christopher Day and his colleagues surveyed and interviewed 300 teachers in 100 schools in the United Kingdom over a 3-year period about their sense of their own effectiveness. They then connected these results to value-added achievement measures. Effectiveness in outcomes was closely connected to teachers' sense of self-efficacy and their commitment to their work and their students. "For commitment to flourish and for teachers to be resilient and effective", the researchers found, teachers needed to have a "strong and enduring sense of efficacy" and to work in morale-building environments of policy, leadership and collegiality (Day, Sammons and Stobart, 2007).

### *Teachers' self-efficacy and job satisfaction*

A number of other studies have also demonstrated positive associations between teachers' self-efficacy and higher levels of student achievement and motivation, and teachers' instructional practices, enthusiasm, commitment, job satisfaction and teaching behaviour (Skaalvik and Skaalvik, 2007; Tschannen-Moran and Woolfolk Hoy, 2001; Tschannen-Moran and Barr, 2004; Caprara et al., 2006). By contrast, lower levels of teachers' self-efficacy have been linked to teachers reporting more difficulties with student misbehaviour, being more pessimistic about student learning, and experiencing higher levels of job-related stress and lower levels of job satisfaction (Caprara et al., 2003; Caprara et al., 2006; Klassen and Chiu, 2010; Collie, Shapka and Perry, 2012). Furthermore, the effects of teachers' self-efficacy appear to know no geographic borders: there is evidence that teachers' self-efficacy is positively related to teachers' job satisfaction across languages and cultures (OECD, 2009).

This positive relationship between teachers' self-efficacy and job satisfaction is also important because there is empirical evidence of the positive association between job satisfaction and job performance across a wide range of work settings. Commitment to a job has an important role in this relationship, as job satisfaction leads to enhanced commitment, which, in turns, leads to better job performance. Moreover, job satisfaction plays a key role in teachers' attitudes and efforts in their daily work with children. Exploring the relationship between teachers' self-efficacy and job satisfaction may thus have implications for teachers' commitment to the school, their performance on the job and, by extension, the academic achievement of students.

Although the described studies show associations between teacher self-efficacy and student achievement, most of these studies did not research the causality of these associations. Caprara et al. (2006) investigated the direction of causality and found that teachers' beliefs about their efficacy affected their job satisfaction and students' academic achievement after accounting for students' previous levels of achievement. Yet Holzberger, Philipp and Kunter (2013) only partially confirmed a causal effect of teachers' self-efficacy on instructional quality; their analyses revealed that instructional quality also affects teacher self-efficacy. Further research is needed to better understand these relationships.

Despite the emerging evidence of the relationship between teachers' self-efficacy and student learning, relatively little is known about how teachers' job satisfaction and self-efficacy are related to each other and to demographic characteristics, such as years of experience, gender, educational attainment and teaching level. Self-efficacy beliefs and job satisfaction are not static: they reflect changes in personal characteristics and circumstances over a lifetime (Klassen and Chiu, 2010).

Research seems to suggest that teachers' self-efficacy is most malleable in the early stage of a teacher's career, after which it increases and becomes more stable as teachers gain experience (Tschannen-Moran and Woolfolk Hoy, 2007; Wolters and Daugherty, 2007). However, Klassen and Chiu (2010) reported a non-linear relationship between teachers' self-efficacy and years of experience, with teacher's self-efficacy increasing with experience among teachers in the early and middle stages of their careers, but declining among teachers in later stages of their careers.

It seems that the middle and late career stages bring their own challenges that can affect self-efficacy and job satisfaction. The combination of successful past experience, verbal support from principals, students, peers and parents, and opportunities to observe successful peers builds teachers' self-efficacy (Tschannen-Moran, Woolfolk Hoy and Hoy, 1998). The relative influence of these sources of self-efficacy is likely to change over the course of a teacher's career, with verbal persuasion and contextual factors having a stronger impact on novice teachers than on veteran teachers (Tschannen-Moran and Woolfolk Hoy, 2007). In one of the few studies researching the relationship between teacher training and self-efficacy, Woolfolk Hoy and Burke Spero (2005) reported a significant increase in teachers' self-efficacy during teacher training, followed by a decline at the end of the first year of teaching.

To get a better idea of what teachers, themselves, see as the greatest challenges they face, TALIS asked teachers about their professional development needs. Across all participating countries, about 22% of teachers, on average, reported

that they need more professional development for teaching students with special needs (Figure 1.10). The second and third most important professional development needs that teachers reported are related to teaching with information and communication technology (19% of teachers) and to using new technologies in the workplace (18% of teachers), two closely related items.

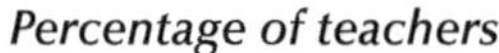

Figure 1.10

**Teachers' needs for professional development**

*Percentage of teachers*

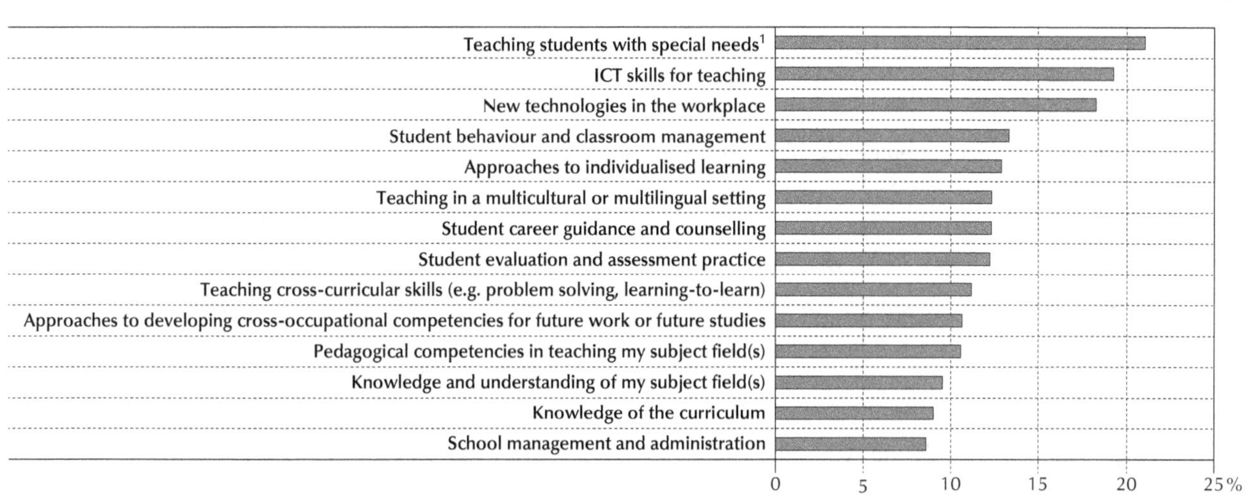



1. Special needs students are not well defined internationally but usually cover those for whom a special learning need has been formally identified because they are mentally, physically or emotionally disadvantaged. Often special needs students are those for whom additional public or private resources (personnel, material or financial) have been provided to support their education. "Gifted students" are not considered to have special needs under the definition used here and in other OECD work. Some teachers perceive all students as unique learners and thus having some special learning needs. For the purpose of this survey, it is important to ensure a more objective judgment of who is a special needs student and who is not. That is why a formal identification is stressed above.

**Source:** OECD (2013), TALIS 2013 complete database, http://stats.oecd.org/index.aspx?datasetcode=talis_2013%20.

**StatLink** http://dx.doi.org/10.1787/888933330450

In Japan and Korea, more than 40% of teachers reported a high level of need for professional development in student career guidance and counselling. Large proportions of teachers in several countries reported the need for more professional development in the area of teaching in a multicultural or multilingual setting. This feeling of unpreparedness is notable in Latin American countries and in the European countries that recently saw rapid increases in the linguistic and cultural diversity in schools, such as Italy and Spain.

### Box 1.3 Another challenge for teachers: Integrating students with an immigrant background

In 2015, more than one million migrants and asylum-seekers – including an unprecedented number of children – braved rough seas and barbed-wire barricades to find safety and a better life in Europe. Are teachers – in Europe and elsewhere – well-equipped to help migrant children integrate into their new communities?

A remarkable finding from the OECD Programme for International Student Assessment (PISA) is the significant cross-country variation in performance between immigrant students and students without an immigrant background, even after accounting for socio-economic status. Even if the culture and the education acquired before migrating have an impact on student performance, the country where immigrant students settle matters more. For example, students from Arabic-speaking countries who settled in the Netherlands score 100 points higher in mathematics than students from the same countries who settled in Qatar, even after accounting for socio-economic differences. Albanian students in Greece score 50 points higher in mathematics than Albanian students of similar socio-economic status in Montenegro, a difference that is very close to the average performance difference between Greece and Montenegro. And while students born in China do better than their non-immigrant peers in virtually every country, that advantage varies widely across countries too. These findings indicate how much public policy can help to integrate immigrant children.

...

Similarly, some countries are better than others at fostering a sense of belonging among immigrant students. In Belgium, Ireland, Luxembourg and Portugal, first-generation immigrant students expressed the most alienation from education systems as compared to students without an immigrant background. Integration unfolds over time in Luxembourg, Norway and Spain, where second-generation immigrant students expressed a stronger sense of belonging at school than first-generation immigrant students. In Australia, Canada, New Zealand and Qatar, the percentages of both first- and second-generation immigrant students who reported that that feel they belong at school were higher than the percentage of non-immigrant students who so reported. All four of these countries adopt highly selective immigration policies.

PISA results also suggest that the well-being of immigrant students is affected not just by cultural differences between the country of origin and the host country, but also by how schools and communities help immigrant students deal with daily problems of living, learning and communicating. For example, almost 90% of students from Iraq who settled in Finland reported feeling like they belong at school, but only 69% of students from Iraq who settled in Denmark reported the same.

The policies and practices countries use to integrate migrant students into schools largely determine whether integration is successful or not. So what can schools and teachers do?

**Provide language instruction quickly**. Combining language and content learning, from as soon as it becomes feasible, has proven to be most effective in integrating children with an immigrant background into education systems. While language assistance is important, it should be in addition to, rather than instead of, regular instruction – regardless of the age of the student or how long ago he or she arrived in the host country.

**Offer high-quality early childhood education**, tailored to language development. If children enter such programmes at the age of 2 or 3 they have a chance of starting school at almost the same level as non-immigrant children. Where such programmes are not available or if migrant families are reluctant to enrol their children, targeted home visits can help families to support their child's learning at home and can also ease entry into appropriate education services.

**Encourage teachers to participate in professional development**. All efforts to integrate migrant children depend on a well-skilled, well-supported teaching force. While many classrooms are now filled with immigrants from a range of backgrounds, often the teachers in these classrooms are unfamiliar with the pedagogical approaches for second-language learning. They are often untrained in recognising the effects of trauma that many immigrant children have endured and in helping these children to overcome them.

**Avoid concentrating immigrant students in the same, disadvantaged schools**. It is common sense, and borne out in the evidence, that schools that struggle to do well for non-immigrant students will struggle even more with a large population of children who cannot speak or understand the language of instruction. Countries that distribute migrant students across a mix of schools achieve better outcomes for all students. A more even distribution also relieves the pressure on schools and teachers when large numbers of immigrant students arrive over a short period of time.

**Re-think education policies**. While ability grouping, grade repetition and tracking are harmful for all students, immigrant students are more likely to be affected by these practices. Language difficulties and cultural differences can be misinterpreted as lack of ability and potential, when this is not the case.

**Reach out to immigrant parents**. While teachers are critical to migrant students' success in school, so are their parents. Students do better when their parents understand the importance of schooling, how the school system works, and how best to support their child's progress through school.

**Source:** OECD (2015), *Immigrant Students at School: Easing the Journey towards Integration*, http://dx.doi.org/ 10.1787/9789264249509-en.

## References


**Ayres, P., S. Dinham** and **W. Sawyer** (2000), *Successful Senior Secondary Teaching*, Australian College of Education, Canberra.

**Bandura, A.** (1995), "Exercise of personal and collective efficacy in changing societies", *Self-efficacy in Changing Societies*, Cambridge University Press, pp 1-45, online publication 2010, http://dx.doi.org/10.1017/CBO9780511527692.

**Baumert** (2011), see www.mpib-berlin.mpg.de/coactiv/en/.

**Berliner, D.C.** (2004), "Describing the behavior and documenting the accomplishments of expert teachers", *Bulletin of Science, Technology, Society*, Vol. 24/3, pp. 200-212.

**Berliner, D.C.** (2001), "Learning about and learning from expert teachers", *International Journal of Educational Research*, Vol. 35/5, pp. 463-482.

**Blömeke, S.** and **S. Delaney** (2012), "Assessment of teacher knowledge across countries: A review of the state of research", *ZDM Mathematics Education*, Vol. 44, pp. 223-247.

**Blömeke, S.** et al. (2008a), "Future teachers' competence to plan a lesson: First results of a six-country study on the efficiency of teacher education", *ZDM Mathematics Education*, Vol. 40, pp. 749-762.

**Blömeke, S.** et al. (2008b), "Effectiveness of teacher education: State of research, measurement issues, and consequences for future studies", *ZDM Mathematics Education*, Vol. 40, pp. 719-734.

**Butler, R.** (2012), "Striving to connect: Extending an achievement goal approach to teacher motivation to include relational goals for teaching", *Journal of Educational Psychology*, Vol. 104/3, pp. 726-742.

**Butler, R.** and **L. Shibaz** (2014), "Striving to connect and striving to learn: Influences of relational and mastery goals for teaching on teacher behaviors and student interest and help seeking", *International Journal of Educational Research*, Vol. 65/0, pp. 41-53.

**Caprara, G.V.** et al. (2006), "Teachers' self-efficacy beliefs as determinants of job satisfaction and students' academic achievement: A study at the school level", *Journal of School Psychology*, Vol. 44/6, pp. 473-490.

**Caprara, G.V.** et al. (2003), "Efficacy beliefs as determinants of teachers' job satisfaction", *Journal of Educational Psychology*, Vol. 95, pp. 821-832.

**Ciani, K. D., J.J. Summers** and **M.A. Easter** (2008), "A 'top-down' analysis of high school teacher motivation", *Contemporary Educational Psychology*, Vol. 33/4, pp. 533-560.

**Collie, R.J., J.D. Shapka** and **N.E. Perry** (2012), "School climate and socio-emotional learning: Predicting teacher stress, job satisfaction, and teaching efficacy", *Journal of Educational Psychology*, Vol. 104/4, pp. 1189-1204.

**Day, C., P. Sammons** and **G. Stobart** (2007), *Teachers Matter: Connecting Work, Lives And Effectiveness*, McGraw-Hill Education, Maidenhead, UK.

**Echazarra, A.** and **D. Salinas** (forthcoming), "How teachers teach and students learn: Strategies for success at school", *OECD Education Working Papers*, OECD Publishing, Paris.

**Education Commission of the States** (2003), "Eight questions on teacher preparation: What does the research say?", Education Commission of the States, Denver, CO.

**Goldhaber, D.** and **D. Brewer** (2000), "Does teacher certification matter? High school teacher certification status and student achievement", *Educational Evaluation and Policy Analysis*, Vol. 22/2, pp. 129-145.

**Gustafsson, J.E.** (2003), "What do we know about effects of school resources on educational results?", *Swedish Economic Policy Review*, Vol. 10, pp. 77-110.

**Hattie, J.** (2003), "Teachers make a difference: Building teacher quality", ACER Annual Conference, Auckland.

**Holzberger, D., A. Philipp** and **M. Kunter** (2014), "Predicting teachers' instructional behaviors: The interplay between self-efficacy and intrinsic needs", *Contemporary Educational Psychology*, Vol. 39/2, pp. 100-111.

**Holzberger, D., A. Philipp** and **M. Kunter** (2013), "How teachers' self-efficacy is related to instructional quality: A longitudinal analysis", *Journal of Educational Psychology*, online first publication, 29 April 2013, http://dx.doi.org/10.1037/a0032198.

**Klassen, R.M.** and **M.M. Chiu** (2010), "Effects on teachers' self-efficacy and job satisfaction: Teacher gender, years of experience, and job stress", *Journal of Educational Psychology*, Vol. 102/3, pp. 741-756.

**König, J.** et al. (2011), "General pedagogical knowledge of future middle school teachers: On the complex ecology of teacher education in the United States, Germany and Taiwan", *Journal of Teacher Education*, Vol. 62, pp. 188-201.

**Kunter, M.** and **J. Baumert** (2006), "Who is the expert? Construct and criteria validity of student and teacher ratings of instruction", *Learning Environments Research*, Vol. 9/3, pp. 231-251.

**Kunter, M.** et al. (2013), "Professional competence of teachers: Effects on instructional quality and student development", *Journal of Educational Psychology*, Vol. 105/3, pp. 805-820.

**Kunter, M.** et al. (2008), "Students' and mathematics teachers' perceptions of teacher enthusiasm and instruction", *Learning and Instruction*, Vol. 18/5, pp. 468-482.

**Lauermann, F.** (2015), "Teacher motivation research and its implications for the instructional process: A technical report and recommendations for an international large-scale assessment of teachers' knowledge and professional competencies", technical paper prepared for the OECD Innovative Teaching for Effective Learning (ITEL) – Phase II Project: A Survey to Profile the Pedagogical Knowledge in the Teaching Profession (ITEL Teacher Knowledge Survey), OECD, Paris.

**Lingard, B., W. Martino, M. Mills** and **M. Bahr** (2002), "Addressing the educational needs of boys: Strategies for schools and teachers", Commonwealth Department of Education, Science and Training, Canberra.

**Monk, D.H.** (1994), "Subject area preparation of secondary mathematics and science teachers and student achievement", *Economics of Education Review*, Vol. 13/2, pp. 125-145.

**Murnane, R.** (1996), "Staffing the Nation's Schools with Skilled Teachers", in E. Hanushek and D. Jorgenson (eds.), *Improving America's Schools: The Role of Incentives*, National Academy Press, Washington, DC.

**OECD** (2015), *Immigrant Students at School: Easing the Journey towards Integration*, OECD Reviews of Migrant Education, OECD Publishing, Paris, http://dx.doi.org/10.1787/9789264249509-en.

**OECD** (2009), *Creating Effective Teaching and Learning Environments: First Results from TALIS*, TALIS, OECD Publishing, Paris, http://dx.doi.org/10.1787/9789264072992-en.

**Rice, J.** (2003), *Teacher Quality: Understanding the Effectiveness of Teacher Attributes*, Economic Policy Institute, Washington, DC.

**Rivkin, S., E. Hanushek** and **J. Kain** (2001), "Teachers, schools, and academic achievement", *Working Paper 6691* (revised), National Bureau of Economic Research, Cambridge, MA.

**Shulman, L.** (1992), "Ways of seeing, ways of knowing, ways of teaching, ways of learning about teaching", *Journal of Curriculum Studies*, Vol. 28, pp. 393-396.

**Shulman, L.** (1987), "Knowledge and teaching: Foundations of the new reform", *Harvard Educational Review*, Vol. 57/1, pp. 1-22.

**Shulman, L.S.** (1986), "Those who understand: Knowledge growth in teaching", *Educational Researcher*, Vol. 15/2, pp. 4-14.

**Skaalvik, E.M.** and **S. Skaalvik** (2007), "Dimensions of teacher self-efficacy and relations with strain factors, perceived collective teacher efficacy, and teacher burnout", *Journal of Educational Psychology*, Vol. 99/3, pp. 611-625.

**Sternberg, R.J.** and **J.A. Horvath** (1995), "A prototype view of expert teaching", *Educational Researcher*, Vol. 24/6, pp. 9-17.

**Thoonen, E.E.J.** et al. (2011), "How to improve teaching practices: The role of teacher motivation, organizational factors, and leadership practices", *Educational Administration Quarterly*, Vol. 47/3, pp. 496-536.

**Thoonen, E.E.J., P.J.C. Sleegers, T.T.D. Peetsma** and **F.J. Oort** (2011), "Can teachers motivate students to learn?" *Educational Studies*, Vol. 37/3, pp. 345-360.

**Tschannen-Moran, M.** and **M. Barr** (2004), "Fostering student achievement: The relationship between collective teacher efficacy and student achievement", *Leadership and Policy in Schools*, Vol. 3/3, pp. 187-207.

**Tschannen-Moran, M.** and **A. Woolfolk Hoy** (2007), "The differential antecedents of self-efficacy beliefs of novice and experienced teachers", *Teaching and Teacher Education*, Vol. 23/6, pp. 944-956.

**Tschannen-Moran, M.** and **A. Woolfolk Hoy** (2001), "Teacher efficacy: Capturing an elusive construct", *Teaching and Teacher Education*, Vol. 17/7, pp. 783-805.

**Tschannen-Moran, M., A. Woolfolk Hoy** and **W.K. Hoy** (1998), "Teacher efficacy: Its meaning and measure", *Review of Educational Research*, Vol. 68, pp. 202-248.

**Voss, T., M. Kunter** and **J. Baumert** (2011), "Assessing teacher candidates' general pedagogical/ psychological knowledge: Test construction and validation", *Journal of Educational Psychology*, Vol. 103/4, pp. 952-969.

**Wayne, A.J.** and **P. Youngs** (2003), "Teacher characteristics and student achievement gains: A review", *Review of Educational Research*, Vol. 73/1, pp. 89-122.

**Wenglinsky, H.** (2002), "How schools matter: The link between teacher practices and student academic performance", Education Policy Analysis Archives, Vol. 10/12.

**Wenglinsky, H.** (2000), *How Teaching Matters: Bringing the Classroom back into Discussions of Teacher Quality*, Policy Information Center Report, Educational Testing Service, Princeton, NJ.

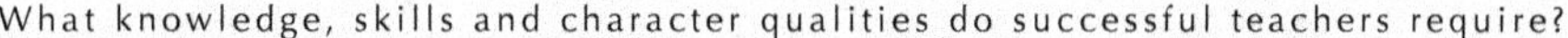

**Westerman, D.A.** (1991), "Expert and novice teacher decision making", *Journal of Teacher Education*, Vol. 42/4, pp. 292-305.

**Wilson, S., R. Floden** and **J. Ferrini-Mundy** (2001), *Teacher Preparation Research: Current Knowledge, Gaps and Recommendations*, University of Washington, Seattle, WA.

**Woessmann, L.** (2003), "Schooling resources, educational institutions and student performance: The international evidence", *Oxford Bulletin of Economics and Statistics*, Vol. 65/2, pp. 117-170.

**Woolfolk Hoy, A.** and **R. Burke Spero** (2005), "Changes in teacher efficacy during the early years of teaching: A comparison of four measures", *Teaching and Teacher Education*, Vol. 21/4, pp. 343-356.

**Wolters, C.A.** and **S.G. Daugherty** (2007), "Goal structures and teachers' sense of efficacy: Their relation and association to teaching experience and academic level", *Journal of Educational Psychology*, Vol. 99/1, pp. 181-193.

# Chapter 2

# WHAT POLICIES CAN HELP TEACHERS ACQUIRE THE KNOWLEDGE AND SKILLS THEY NEED?

This chapter defines teacher professionalism, and describes some of the policies and practices that help develop and enhance it. These include fostering a collaborative culture in schools, providing induction programmes and peer mentoring, focusing on student assessment, strengthening the links between teacher appraisal and professional development, involving teachers in developing professional standards, and engaging teachers in education reform. The chapter highlights examples of effective policies and practices from around the world.

**Note regarding Israel**

The statistical data for Israel are supplied by and under the responsibility of the relevant Israeli authorities. The use of such data by the OECD is without prejudice to the status of the Golan Heights, East Jerusalem and Israeli settlements in the West Bank under the terms of international law.

Historically, the concept of professionalism referred to the level of autonomy and internal regulation exercised by members of an occupation in providing services to society (Evans, 2008). Early researchers evaluated whether changes in a particular livelihood were a result of external forces or were due to the internal motivation and efforts of the members of the profession itself. In 18th- and 19th-century Europe, the distinction between occupations and professions lay in the level to which a profession required special knowledge, a formal code of conduct and a mandate to carry out particular services given out by the state, which served as "...the guarantor of legal order [and] the promoter of culture..." (Siegrist, 2015). Over time, the classic definition of the professions was expanded, and university professors and upper secondary teachers were recognised as the experts for education, aesthetics and morality (Siegrist, 2015).

In the 20th century, the professionalisation of teaching was stymied by the growing standardisation of curricula and, with it, the emergence of external accountability. The expansion of education opportunities around the world over the course of the century led to an increase in the number of teachers and scripted lesson plans.

At the turn of the 21st century, however, there was renewed focus on teacher professionalism as an approach to education reform (Darling-Hammond and Lieberman, 2013): as improving teacher quality became viewed as the key to student achievement, teacher professionalism gained greater prominence. Indeed, today teachers' continuous professional development is widely seen as essential for improving teachers' performance and effectiveness, and for enhancing their commitment to their work. Nonetheless, the meaning of teacher professionalism, and the nature and extent of professionalism practices, varies significantly across countries. Varied approaches to professionalism may reflect cultural and historical differences, or differences in national and local policy priorities.

## WHAT TEACHER PROFESSIONALISM LOOKS LIKE AROUND THE WORLD

It is instructive to turn to a few high-performing education systems to see what teacher professionalism means on the ground. Interestingly, there is almost just as much variation in approaches to teacher professionalism among high performers as in the rest of the world. Hong Kong (China), for example, has introduced greater teacher autonomy than its neighbours in East Asia. As the OECD notes in its recent *Lessons from PISA* publication (OECD, 2014a), school administrators and teachers in Hong Kong are given the freedom to customise the curriculum, materials and methods. This breadth and depth of autonomy has fostered high teacher professional self-esteem and the internal motivation for continuous professional development. Even with low-performing schools, the government does not intervene in school management; it relies instead on the decision-making power of the school administration and teachers (OECD, 2014a). By contrast, in Shanghai (China), the municipal government designs the policies, manages the schools and improves instruction (OECD, 2014a). Teachers in Shanghai are comprehensively and rigorously trained in pre-service programmes and subsequent regular professional development activities (OECD, 2014a). They are expected to implement the standards and curricular approaches defined by the government and generally have a narrower space for interpretation of curricular objectives (Lai and Lo, 2007).

High-quality teachers and school leaders have formed the cornerstone of the Singapore education system and are a major reason for its high performance. Singapore has developed a comprehensive system for selecting, training, compensating and developing teachers and principals, thereby creating tremendous capacity at the point of education delivery (OECD, 2014a). In Singapore, professional development is defined by apprenticeship, mentoring and collaborative learning environments (National Institute of Education, 2009). Much professional development is school-based, led by staff developers who identify teaching-based problems or introduce new practices. This accords the teaching profession greater autonomy over professional development and facilitates a teacher-led culture of professional excellence (OECD, 2014a). Korea – another East Asian high performer in PISA – relies on the teacher candidate-selection process, pre-service teacher training and national evaluation process – all of which serve to ensure that only the best and the brightest join the ranks of teachers (OECD, 2014a).

In Europe and North America, the usual high performers in PISA – Australia, Canada, Finland, the Netherlands and Sweden – have traditionally been commended for their strong teacher professionalisation practices and the latitude given to teachers to customise their teaching (OECD, 2013a). Most notably, researchers argued that Finland's early success in PISA was explained by the fact that it "...publicly recognizes the value of its teachers and trusts their professional judgements in schools..." (Sahlberg, 2010). Similarly, Webb et al. (2004) document how Finnish teachers tend to emphasise autonomous decision making in their own conceptions of their professionalism.

These differences in the degree of autonomy that teachers are granted suggest that the impact of that autonomy depends on the context. In countries in which teacher training and selection procedures ensure a well-prepared and independent

teaching workforce, autonomy will allow creativity and innovation to flourish; in other cases, autonomy may lead to wrong decisions. Even when teacher quality is similar, the available evidence suggests that autonomy has a positive impact when it is given in return for accountability.

The OECD TALIS survey established a conceptual framework for teacher professionalism. This framework describes teacher professionalism through teachers' knowledge base, autonomy and peer networks. In order to measure how well education systems support teachers' professionalism in each of these domains, TALIS calculates the average number of best practices, as reported by teachers (Box 2.1). Each of the domains of teacher professionalism is scaled from 0 to 5, with 5 representing a theoretical maximum where all practices within the domain are observed. The overall index of teacher professionalism is the sum of the values in the three domains, ranging from a theoretical minimum of 0 to a possible maximum of 15. In reality, most teachers find themselves in environments where these practices are partially observed.

### Box 2.1 The TALIS index of teacher professionalism

In constructing the three TALIS scales of professionalism, three composite, additive scales were created. These scales weigh each factor equally and create an additive scale that ranges from 0-5. The composite additive approach, which is based on tangible, observed practices, is more appropriate for teacher professionalism than other approaches, such as confirmatory factor analysis or structural equation modelling, which rely on inter-item correlations to capture a latent construct (such as, for example, job satisfaction). The sub-indices are based on reports from teachers and principals on:

1. Knowledge-base best practices – drawn from TALIS 2013 teacher questionnaire
   - pre-service formal education
   - participation in formal teacher-education programme
   - breadth of content covered in teacher-education programme
   - support for in-service professional learning
   - types of support provided for ongoing professional development during and outside working hours (time, monetary, non-monetary)
   - participation in long-term professional development
   - support for practitioner research
   - participation in practitioner or action-research
2. Autonomy – drawn from TALIS 2013 principal questionnaire
   - decision making over curriculum choices
   - decision making over learning materials
   - decision making over course content
   - decision making over assessment policies
   - decision making over discipline policies
3. Peer networks – drawn from TALIS 2013 teacher questionnaire
   - participation in a formal induction programme
   - participation in formal mentoring programme
   - received peer feedback on teaching based on direct observation
   - development of a professional development plan
   - participation in network supporting teacher professional development

The obvious question is: To what extent does teacher professionalism translate into better teaching and, ultimately, better learning outcomes for students? Figure 2.1 plots system-level values of the TALIS teacher professionalism index against student performance in the PISA 2012 mathematics assessment. The trend line suggests that there is a weak, positive relationship between the overall values on the teacher professionalism index and an education system's learning outcomes.

Figure 2.1

**PISA scores and overall teacher professionalism**

*Lower secondary teachers*

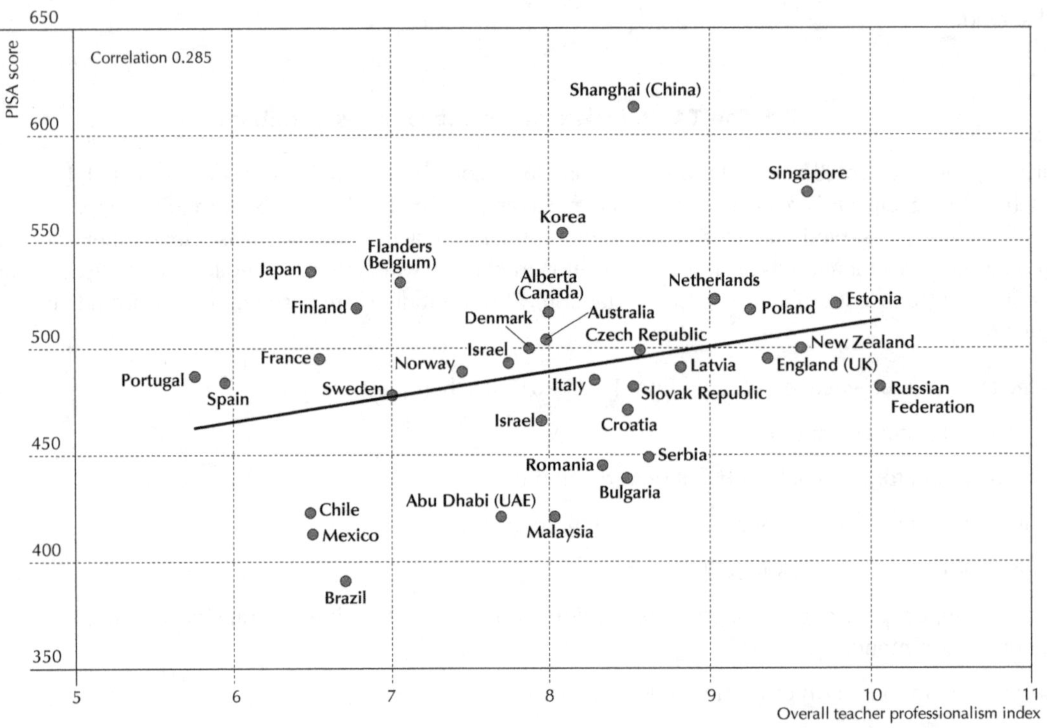


**Sources:** OECD, TALIS 2013 complete database (http://stats.oecd.org/index.aspx?datasetcode=talis_2013%20); OECD (2014), *PISA 2012 Results in Focus: What 15-year-olds Know and What They Can Do with What They Know*, www.oecd.org/pisa/keyfindings/pisa-2012-results-overview.pdf.

StatLink http://dx.doi.org/10.1787/888933330465

The lack of a strong relationship may be due to the complexity and diversity of teacher professionalism included in the index, and suggests that not all of facets of teacher professionalism are equally efficient. Thus, a more detailed analysis would be required to identify which facets have the strongest impact on student performance. One thing is clear however: because teacher professionalism appears, among OECD countries at least, to be unrelated to levels of expenditure on education, the weak relationship between teachers' professionalism and student performance is unrelated to the level of resources invested in education.

## TEACHER PROFESSIONALISM ACROSS COUNTRIES

Teacher professionalism varies across countries and economies both in terms of the overall level of teacher professionalism within the education system and the domain of professionalism the country/economy emphasises. Figure 2.2 shows the overall level of teacher professionalism in each education system, broken down by the value of each domain. Overall values range from a maximum of 10.1 in the Russian Federation to a minimum of 5.8 in Portugal. This distribution suggests that, in general, teachers in the Russian Federation are exposed to two of every three best practices, while those in Portugal and in countries towards the bottom end of the spectrum are exposed to slightly more than one out of three.

Because teacher professionalism is a composite index, countries and economies with the highest overall values on the teacher professionalism index generally have high values in all three domains. As the figure shows, the education systems with the highest values on the composite index are Estonia, New Zealand, the Russian Federation and Singapore. Seven of the ten education systems with the highest overall professionalism are located in Europe, while two (New Zealand and Singapore) are outside of Europe. The three Latin American countries (Brazil, Chile and Mexico) score at the lower end of the overall index, while Portugal and Spain show the lowest levels of teacher professionalism on the composite index among all the systems surveyed by TALIS.

Figure 2.2 lists each system's value in each domain and codes their values along a spectrum from zero to five (at the high end). In general, East Asian, Middle Eastern and Latin American systems grant less autonomy to teachers. This would suggest that the degree of decision making and control over school processes that teachers are accorded may be partly influenced by cultural norms.

Figure 2.2

**Teacher professionalism index, by country**

*Lower secondary teachers*

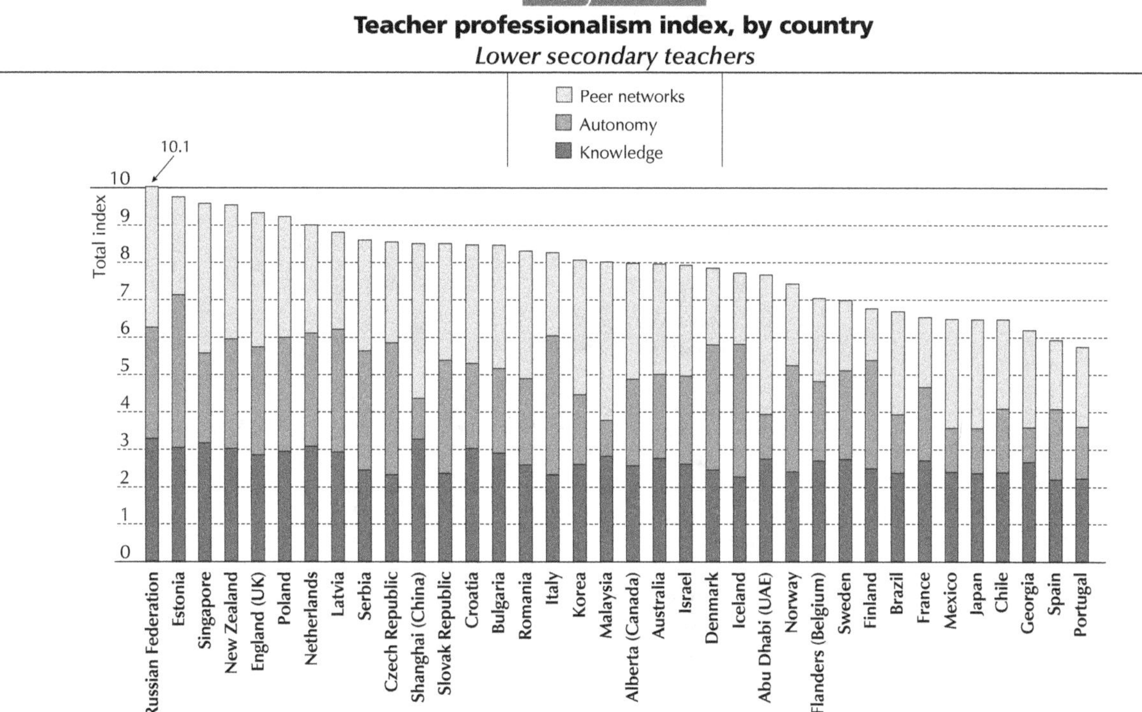


*Countries are ranked in descending order of their overall value on the teacher professionalism index.*

**Source:** OECD (2013), TALIS 2013 complete database, http://stats.oecd.org/index.aspx?datasetcode=talis_2013%20.

StatLink http://dx.doi.org/10.1787/888933330471

Meanwhile, only two of the education systems that emphasise peer networks are located in Europe, namely England (United Kingdom) and Romania. Peer networks tend to be emphasised most among East Asian countries and economies. The few Latin American and Middle Eastern systems that participated in TALIS also score highest on the peer networks scale. This finding implies a cultural difference in the degree to which countries promote networking and peer feedback among teachers, with East Asian countries and economies such as Malaysia, Shanghai (China) and Singapore among the systems with the highest values on this measure.

## THE IMPACT OF TEACHER PROFESSIONALISM

To what extent does teacher professionalism, as measured by this index, make a difference? Table 2.1 shows a teacher's predicted percentile in the distribution of all teachers, estimated by his or her overall score on the teacher professionalism index. The table indicates where, among all teachers, a given teacher would be expected to rank if he/she benefitted from only one best practice, compared to those who benefit from five or ten best practices that the OECD identifies as important. Teachers with a value of only one on the overall index are expected to fall among the bottom third of all teachers in terms of their perceived status, self-efficacy and satisfaction with their profession and work environment.

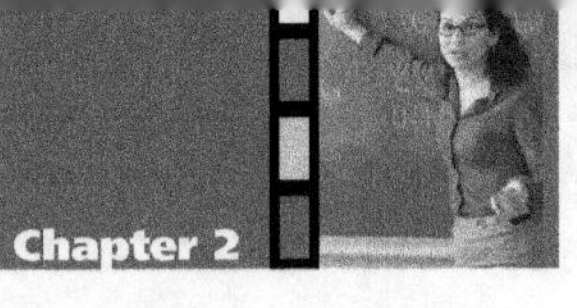



In contrast, teachers with a value of five on the overall professionalism index are in the 40th to 51st percentile of all teachers in terms of all outcomes. At the top end of the spectrum, teachers with values of ten on the overall index, which corresponds to benefitting from two-thirds of the identified best practices, are likely to rank among the top half of all teachers.

Table 2.1

**National means on teacher professionalism domains**

*Lower secondary teachers*

| | Knowledge | Autonomy | Networks |
|---|---|---|---|
| **Abu Dhabi (United Arab Emirates)** | 2.8 | 1.2 | 3.7 |
| **Alberta (Canada)** | 2.6 | 2.3 | 3.1 |
| **Australia** | 2.8 | 2.2 | 3.0 |
| **Brazil** | 2.4 | 1.6 | 2.8 |
| **Bulgaria** | 2.9 | 2.3 | 3.3 |
| **Chile** | 2.4 | 1.7 | 2.4 |
| **Croatia** | 3.0 | 2.3 | 3.2 |
| **Czech Republic** | 2.3 | 3.5 | 2.7 |
| **Denmark** | 2.5 | 3.4 | 2.1 |
| **England (United Kingdom)** | 2.9 | 2.9 | 3.6 |
| **Estonia** | 3.1 | 4.1 | 2.6 |
| **Finland** | 2.5 | 2.9 | 1.4 |
| **Flanders (Belgium)** | 2.7 | 2.1 | 2.2 |
| **France** | 2.7 | 2.0 | 1.9 |
| **Georgia** | 2.7 | 0.9 | 2.6 |
| **Iceland** | 2.3 | 3.6 | 1.9 |
| **Israel** | 2.6 | 2.4 | 3.0 |
| **Italy** | 2.3 | 3.7 | 2.2 |
| **Japan** | 2.4 | 1.2 | 2.9 |
| **Korea** | 2.6 | 1.9 | 3.6 |
| **Latvia** | 2.9 | 3.3 | 2.6 |
| **Malaysia** | 2.8 | 1.0 | 4.3 |
| **Mexico** | 2.4 | 1.2 | 2.9 |
| **Netherlands** | 3.1 | 3.0 | 2.9 |
| **New Zealand** | 3.0 | 2.9 | 3.6 |
| **Norway** | 2.4 | 2.9 | 2.2 |
| **Poland** | 3.0 | 3.1 | 3.2 |
| **Portugal** | 2.2 | 1.4 | 2.1 |
| **Romania** | 2.6 | 2.3 | 3.4 |
| **Russian Federation** | 3.3 | 3.0 | 3.8 |
| **Serbia** | 2.5 | 3.2 | 3.0 |
| **Shanghai (China)** | 3.3 | 1.1 | 4.2 |
| **Singapore** | 3.2 | 2.4 | 4.0 |
| **Slovak Republic** | 2.4 | 3.0 | 3.1 |
| **Spain** | 2.2 | 1.9 | 1.9 |
| **Sweden** | 2.7 | 2.4 | 1.9 |

Source: OECD (2013), TALIS 2013 complete database, http://stats.oecd.org/index.aspx?datasetcode=talis_2013%20.
StatLink http://dx.doi.org/10.1787/888933330603

In concrete terms, it appears that using even a few best practices matters more for teachers who do not already benefit from any of them than for teachers who use at least two out of three of the best practices. As Figure 2.3 shows, teachers who benefit from fewer than two best practices of teacher professionalism are likely to rank among the bottom third of all teachers in terms of their perceived status and satisfaction; they are much less likely to report that they believe teaching is valued in society and that they are satisfied in their work environment and with their profession, in general. They are also less likely to be confident about their teaching (self-efficacy), although the impact is less pronounced: even teachers in schools that use fewer than two best practices fall within the 35th percentile of all teachers. In contrast, those benefitting from roughly two out of three practices are likely to be in the top half of the distribution, all other factors held constant.

Figure 2.3

**Teacher professionalism and teacher outcomes**

*Lower secondary teachers*

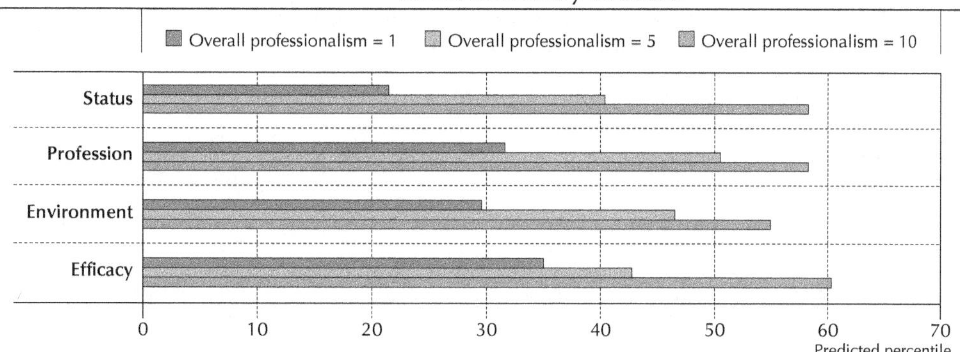


**Note:** The baseline is set as one best practice on the total professionalism index because very few teachers in the dataset had a value of 0 on the overall index. The small sample made predictions on that population unreliable.
**Source:** OECD (2013), TALIS 2013 complete database, http://stats.oecd.org/index.aspx?datasetcode=talis_2013%20.
StatLink http://dx.doi.org/10.1787/888933330483

## FORMULATING EXPECTATIONS

To build teacher professionalism, policy makers and the profession itself must establish clearly and concisely what teachers are expected to know and be able to do. This framework will guide initial teacher education, teacher certification, teachers' ongoing professional development and career advancement, and can be used to assess the effectiveness of each.

Teachers' work and the knowledge and skills that they need to be effective should reflect the learning objectives that schools aim to achieve. There needs to be profession-wide standards and a shared understanding of what counts as accomplished teaching. The profile should be evidence-based and built on the teaching profession's definitions of teacher competencies and standards of performance. It should reflect the broad range of competencies that teachers need to be effective practitioners in modern schools. It should encompass strong subject-matter knowledge, pedagogical skills, the capacity to work effectively with a wide range of students and colleagues, contributions to the school and the wider profession, and the teacher's capacity to continue developing. The profile could delineate the different levels of performance appropriate to beginning teachers, experienced teachers, and those with greater responsibilities. Not least, the profile should emphasise the demonstrated attainment of key knowledge, skills and competencies for effective professional practice.

## PROFESSIONAL DEVELOPMENT

### *How well-prepared teachers feel*

TALIS data show that a majority of teachers has received formal content and pedagogical training and a practical component for some or all of the subjects they currently teach. In general, teachers report that their formal education prepared them well for their work as teachers (Figure 2.4). On average, 93% of teachers reported being well or very well prepared to teach the content of the subjects they teach, and 89% feel well or very well prepared in terms of the pedagogy and the practical components of the subjects they teach.

On average, 72% of teachers reported having received formal education that included content for all the subjects they currently teach. A further 23% of teachers reported having received prior content training for at least some of their subjects. Meanwhile, an average of 70% of secondary teachers reported that their formal education included pedagogy training for all the subjects they teach, and nearly one in four (23%) reported participating in this training for some of the subjects they teach. The proportions are similar for practical components: on average, 67% of teachers reported that their formal education included classroom practice in all of the subjects they teach, while 22% reported classroom practice in some of the subjects they teach.

What is it about a teacher's formal education, then, that makes the teacher feel more or less prepared for teaching? Results from TALIS analyses suggest that not only does a teacher's formal education, including teacher initial education, help him or her feel better prepared for work as a teacher, but the specific elements included in that training, such as content and pedagogical training, and classroom practice, can make a significant difference as well.

Figure 2.4

**Teachers' feelings of preparedness for teaching**

*Percentage of lower secondary teachers who reported feeling "very well prepared", "well prepared", "somewhat prepared" or "not at all prepared" for the content and the pedagogy of the subject(s) they teach and whether these were included in their formal education and training*

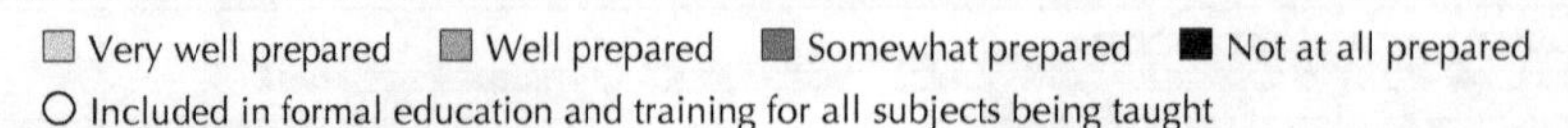

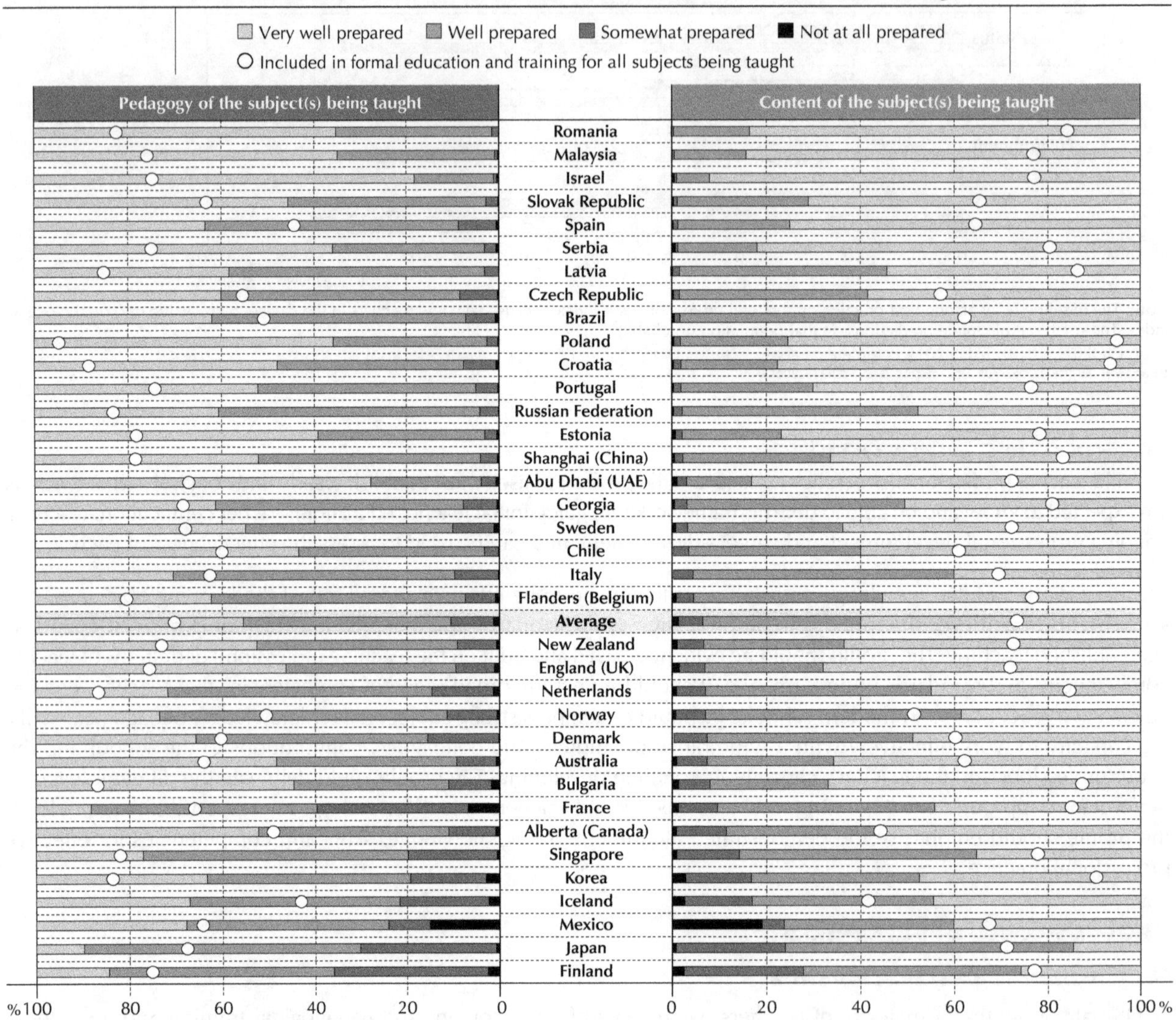
Very well prepared
Well prepared
Somewhat prepared
Not at all prepared
Included in formal education and training for all subjects being taught
Pedagogy of the subject(s) being taught
Content of the subject(s) being taught
Romania
Malaysia
Israel
Slovak Republic
Spain
Serbia
Latvia
Czech Republic
Brazil
Poland
Croatia
Portugal
Russian Federation
Estonia
Shanghai (China)
Abu Dhabi (UAE)
Georgia
Sweden
Chile
Italy
Flanders (Belgium)
Average
New Zealand
England (UK)
Netherlands
Norway
Denmark
Australia
Bulgaria
France
Alberta (Canada)
Singapore
Korea
Iceland
Mexico
Japan
Finland
%100
80
60
40
20
0
0
20
40
60
80
100%

*Countries are ranked in ascending order, based on the percentage of teachers who reported feeling "not at all prepared" or "somewhat prepared" for the content of the subject(s) being taught.*

**Source:** OECD (2013), TALIS 2013 complete database, http://stats.oecd.org/index.aspx?datasetcode=talis_2013%20.

StatLink http://dx.doi.org/10.1787/888933330493

## *Approaches to professional development*

Much of the focus of teacher development has been on initial teacher education – the knowledge and skills that teachers acquire before starting work as a teacher. Most of the resources for teacher development have been allocated to pre-service education, and this is the phase that is most intensely debated within countries. In a number of countries, the initial qualification that teachers earn is a key determinant of their career path. However, given the rapid changes in education, the potentially long careers that many teachers have, and the need for updating skills, teachers' development must be viewed in terms of lifelong learning, with initial teacher education conceived as providing the foundation for ongoing learning, rather than producing ready-made professionals.

Effective professional development is continuous. It includes training, practice and feedback, and provides adequate time and follow-up support. Successful programmes involve teachers in learning activities that are similar to those they will use with their students, and encourage the development of teachers' learning communities. A key strategy involves

finding ways for teachers to share their expertise and experience systematically. There is growing interest in ways to build cumulative knowledge across the profession, for example by strengthening connections between research and practice, and encouraging schools to develop as learning organisations.

There is a wide variety of questions in TALIS that ask teachers about their prior participation in professional development activities. TALIS distinguishes between:

- The kinds of traditional professional development activities in which teachers have long participated: conferences, workshops, in-service training, and qualification programmes. They are referred to as "non-school embedded" professional development. Overall, teachers report that they have participated in these kinds of activities more than other kinds of professional development.
- Activities that are more closely aligned with professional development literature, indicating that ongoing, intensive and collaborative activities (referred to here as "school embedded" professional development) have a greater impact on teaching practice. These kinds of activities include participating in professional development networks, undertaking collaborative research on problems of practice, peer observation and coaching.

While teachers in most countries report participating in non-school embedded professional development more often, the general trend is that the greater the participation in one type of professional development activity, the less the participation in the other type. Results from TALIS also suggest that school-embedded professional development activities seem to have a greater impact on teachers' self-efficacy.

There are substantial challenges in ensuring that all teachers – and not only the most motivated ones – are lifelong learners, and in linking individual teachers' development to school needs.

Three broad strategies for professional development are evident among TALIS-participating countries:

- Entitlement-based, which generally results from collective bargaining agreements that stipulate that teachers are entitled to certain amounts of released time and/or financial support to undertake recognised professional development activities.
- Incentive-based, which links professional development to needs identified through a teacher-appraisal process, and/or recognises participation in professional development as a requirement for salary increases or assuming new roles.
- School-based, which links individual teacher development with school-improvement needs.

The three strategies are not necessarily mutually exclusive, although the starting points of the entitlement- and incentive-based approaches tend to be the individual teacher rather than the whole school.

A comprehensive approach to professional development would encompass all three strategies. Providing teachers with agreed levels of released time or financial support for professional development is an explicit recognition of the importance of professional development and a way of enabling teachers to participate. But it is also important for teachers to see the value of participating, to understand that it is an important part of their professional role, and to see the "entitlement" provision as the minimum extent of their participation rather than the maximum. This is most likely to occur when teachers can see a clear link between professional development activities, improvements in their own practice, student progress, and overall school improvement.

### *Fragmentation and limitations*

Although professional development is increasingly woven into policy, it often seems to be fragmented and limited in scope. The three broad strategies described above attempt to stimulate the demand for professional development activities, but they are not always matched by reforms on the supply side. In a number of countries, the use of public funding for professional development activities is restricted to programmes provided by a few organisations, notably teacher-education institutions or agencies specialising in professional development. This can reduce the incentives for innovation and improvement in these programmes, especially in those countries where participation in professional development activities is mandated. It is important to encourage a range of professional development providers, ensure that quality standards are met, and disseminate good practice.

Professional development can also appear fragmented from the individual teacher's perspective. The development of clear teacher profiles and standards of performance at different stages of the teaching career will help to provide a purpose and a framework for professional development, as well as criteria against which the results can be assessed. Teacher portfolios can also allow teachers to keep track of professional development activities in a more systematic manner.

In general, there is still very little understanding about the nature and extent of professional development activities. Activities labelled as "professional development" are diverse, and the outcomes are highly dependent on the particular circumstances in which those activities are undertaken. (For an international review of literature about teacher professional development, see Villegas-Reimers [2003]).

### *The hallmarks of effective programmes*

The most effective forms of professional development seem to be those that focus on clearly articulated priorities, provide ongoing school-based support to classroom teachers, deal with subject-matter content as well as instruction strategies and classroom-management techniques, and create opportunities for teachers to observe, experience and try new teaching methods.

Effective professional development activities forge a close connection between teachers' own development, their teaching responsibilities and their school's goals. A frequently heard criticism of many professional development programmes is that they treat teachers' professional development as an activity distinct from teachers' daily work, which both limits the effectiveness of these programmes and reduces the chances for schools to benefit from informal learning (Education Commission of the States, 2004).

Encouraging schools to become learning organisations requires that teachers have: the *motivation* to create new professional knowledge; the *opportunity* to engage actively in innovation; the *skills* to test the validity of innovations; and the *mechanisms* for transferring the validated innovations rapidly within their school and into other schools (Hargreaves, 2003). Targeted professional development activities can be an important source of ideas and techniques for building these features in schools. Perhaps even more important are skilled school leaders who are able to build a climate of collegiality and improvement within schools, and systems of teacher evaluation and career development that recognise and reward teachers who innovate, share their learning, and help achieve school goals.

TALIS asked teachers whether their professional development covered each of 14 specific topics (such as pedagogical competencies in teaching the subject, student evaluation and assessment practices, approaches to individual learning, and teaching students with special needs), and if so whether that professional development had a positive impact on their teaching. This self-reported measure of effectiveness is important because teachers' perception of the effectiveness of certain professional development activities may affect their future participation in such activities.

Although the reported participation rates in professional development vary widely across the different areas of focus (between 16% and 73% of teachers, on average, reported that they participated in professional development covering at least one of these areas), teachers generally indicated that their professional development has a moderate or large positive impact on their teaching, regardless of the area covered (between 76% and 91% of teachers, on average, reported that their professional development in these areas had a positive impact on their teaching).

However, Figure 2.5 tells a more nuanced story. First, it shows that larger proportions of teachers, on average, reported that they had undertaken professional development focused on the content (73%) or pedagogical knowledge (68%) of the subject they teach rather than in the areas identified by TALIS as emerging competency areas and areas where there is a shortage of skills. For example, 16% of teachers reported that they had participated in professional development on teaching in a multicultural setting, and around 33% of teachers participated in professional development on teaching students with special needs.

Second, teachers are less likely to report a moderate or large positive impact on their teaching from professional development in these emerging competency areas. Some 77% of teachers reported a moderate or large positive impact on their teaching from professional development activities that focused on teaching students with special needs or teaching in a multicultural or multilingual setting. In contrast, 91% of teachers who participated in professional development in subject-matter content and 87% of teachers who participated in such activities focusing on pedagogy reported such positive impact on their teaching.

Individual teacher development, in turn, needs to be associated with school improvement. To be most effective, professional development programmes should be co-ordinated at the school level so that teachers are aware of the learning goals pursued by their colleagues and potential areas for collaboration. Such joint efforts can contribute to establishing learning communities. Schools that associate the individual teacher's needs with the school's priorities, and that also manage to provide the corresponding professional development activities, are likely to perform well.

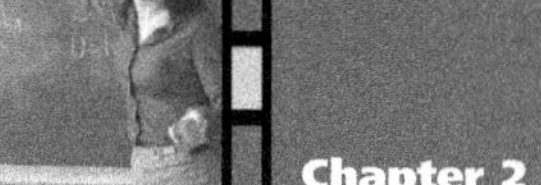


Schools can learn from the strengths of effective teachers and implement professional development programmes that address their weaknesses. Given the important role that school leaders play in linking teacher appraisal results with teacher and school development, school leaders themselves should be well-trained in this task.

Figure 2.5

**Content and impact of professional development activities**

*Percentage of lower secondary teachers who reported having participated in professional development with the following content in the 12 months prior to the survey and who reported a moderate or large positive impact of this professional development on their teaching[1]*

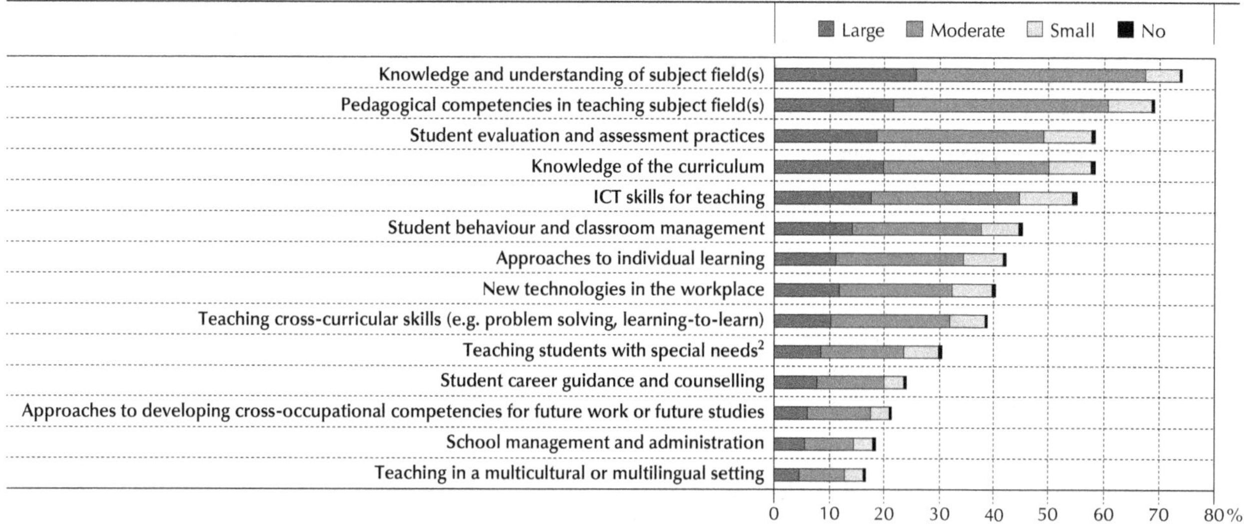


1. The percentages presented in this graph do not have the same denominator. The percentages presented on the perceived impact are based on answers from teachers who indicated that the topic was covered in their professional development activities, while the percentages of teachers who reported that the topic was covered in their professional development activities are based on answers from all the teachers who reported that they participated in professional development activities.

2. Special needs students are not well defined internationally but usually cover those for whom a special learning need has been formally identified because they are mentally, physically or emotionally disadvantaged. Often, special needs students are those for whom additional public or private resources (personnel, material or financial) have been provided to support their education. "Gifted students" are not considered to have special needs under the definition used here and in other OECD work. Some teachers perceive all students as unique learners and thus having some special learning needs. For the purpose of this survey, it is important to ensure a more objective judgment of who is a special needs student and who is not. That is why a formal identification is stressed above.

*Items are ranked in descending order, based on the perceived impact of the topic included in the professional development activities.*

**Source:** OECD (2013), TALIS 2013 complete database, http://stats.oecd.org/index.aspx?datasetcode=talis_2013%20.

**StatLink** http://dx.doi.org/10.1787/888933330506

### Box 2.2 Teacher professional learning in high-performing systems

A new report, *Beyond PD: Teacher Professional Learning in High-Performing Systems*, examines professional learning in four high-performing systems to show how other systems around the world can develop and implement effective teacher development and professional learning programmes.

The study, conducted by *Learning First*, examined teacher professional learning in four high-performing systems: Shanghai (China), Hong Kong (China), Singapore and British Columbia (Canada). While these systems are quite different, a similar strategy ensures that effective collaborative professional learning is built into the daily lives of teachers and school leaders in all of these systems. This is achieved through:

- Greater precision in the delivery of teacher development in schools based on an improvement cycle that is common across all teacher professional learning.
- A system-wide strategy that places a greater emphasis on teacher development that extends well beyond traditional professional-development policies. School accountability, leadership development and school resourcing all ensure that the quality and precision of teacher development in schools is high and continually improving.

...

**Focus on an improvement cycle**

The strategic objective in these systems requires all professional learning to be centred on an improvement cycle that is always tied to student learning. The cycle orients professional learning around the following steps:

- Assess students' learning to identify their next stage of learning (at either an individual or school level).
- Develop the teaching practices that provide for the next stage of student learning (and be clear about what evidence supports this).
- Evaluate the impact of new teaching practices on student learning so that teachers can further refine their practice.

This anchors all teacher professional learning in student learning. Professional learning topics are chosen based on students' greatest needs, and improvements in teaching and learning are evaluated. When applied properly, this method links professional learning to improvements in student learning and to teachers' own needs.

**What makes these systems effective?**

To operationalise an improvement cycle, these four systems use professional learning programmes, like mentoring and learning communities, that encourage and require teacher collaboration and feedback. Professional learning programmes like these are popular around the world, but have mixed results and are often ineffective.

In isolation, an improvement cycle is insufficient for sustained reform. To make the cycle effective requires a broad strategy with strong linkages between how leadership roles are structured, how resources are allocated, and the focus of evaluation and accountability measures. High-performing systems transform the improvement cycle into a culture of continuous professional learning that, in time, turns schools into true learning organisations.

These four systems did not just change single, isolated policies to improve professional learning; they thought about the overall strategy for change. They show that to make teacher professional learning effective, reforms must extend well beyond traditional teacher-development policies. These high-performing systems take a comprehensive approach that includes:

**A reform strategy**: Such a strategy regards effective professional learning as the main catalyst of school improvement. It is a change strategy that recognises that to develop new professional learning and teaching practices in schools, new practices must be continually developed and reinforced. To achieve this, these systems are much more explicit about what constitutes effective professional learning and how schools are to improve. They create clear objectives for developing leaders and for ensuring that schools and other parts of the education system are evaluated and held accountable for improvement and effective professional learning.

**Developing leaders**: In these high-performing systems, it is recognised that new leadership is required to change schools and improve teaching. New leadership positions have been created for teachers to lead teacher professional learning. These teachers are regularly trained alongside school principals so that each school has multiple leaders to continually change practice. They work closely with school principals and ensure that teachers' individual and collective professional learning is meeting school objectives. These include master teachers who develop professional learning in their subject area and in-school professional learning leaders.

**Evaluation and accountability**: Too often discussions about education reform have created a false distinction between development and accountability policies. Systems focus accountability on student outcomes, but then leave it up to schools to determine how to achieve those goals. But for these high-performing systems, evaluation and accountability are integral to the success of professional learning in schools. This is because evaluation and accountability focus not only on student performance, but also on the quality of instruction and professional learning.

A broader focus on accountability does not mean a weakening of consequences for poor performance. On the contrary, district leaders in British Columbia (Canada) hold school leaders accountable for the quality of professional learning in their schools. Teachers in Shanghai (China) are not promoted unless they can demonstrate that they work collaboratively. Similarly, mentors are not promoted unless the teachers they mentor improve. As teachers and school leaders move up their career tracks in Singapore, how they develop other teachers' skills is given increasingly greater weight in their performance review. This reinforces the importance of teacher professional learning to school improvement, and ensures that the quality of teacher development continually improves.

...



 

**Resourcing and creating time:** A common problem that hinders the development of effective professional learning in many systems is a lack of time. Teachers simply do not have sufficient time in the day for professional learning. High-performing systems, however, ensure that sufficient time is available. The average teacher in Shanghai (China) teaches for only 10-12 hours per week. Considerable time is allocated to professional learning. But Shanghai is an outlier even among high-performing systems. For example, in British Columbia (Canada), huge advances have been made with only 1-2 periods per week allocated to formal professional learning. Even this modest difference has enabled much more professional learning within and between classes during the school week.

**Source:** Jensen B., J. Sonnemann, K. Roberts-Hull and A. Hunter (2016), *Beyond PD: Teacher Professional Learning in High-Performing Systems*, www.ncee.org/beyondpd/. This report was authored by Learning First (www.learningfirst.org.au) and commissioned by the Bill and Melinda Gates Foundation and the National Center on Education and the Economy.

## POLICIES TO SUPPORT TEACHER PROFESSIONALISM

### *Prioritising approaches that matter most*

Teachers in TALIS reported less participation in the kinds of professional development activities that are usually considered to be the most effective. For example, teachers reported participating less often in school-embedded professional development that involves teacher collaboration on activities within the school. These differences matter, because participation in school-embedded professional development activities is positively associated with teachers' reports of the impact of professional development activities on their teaching. By contrast, participation in non-school embedded professional development is negatively associated with such impact.

While teachers may acquire new knowledge and skills by participating in professional development activities, whether or not they use what they learn in their own classrooms depends on their own beliefs and the school environment. Results from TALIS show that teachers' beliefs, such as feelings of preparedness, self-efficacy, constructivist pedagogical beliefs, and satisfaction with performance, are associated with self-reports that professional development activities have an impact on teaching. However, the relationship between these beliefs and the reported impact of professional development is not always linear. When teachers report very low or very high levels of self-efficacy, they may be less likely to use new knowledge and skills in their classrooms. Teachers with moderate levels of these beliefs are the most likely to use the knowledge and skills acquired through professional development activities.

In addition, school conditions, such as teacher co-operation and the presence of instructionally focused leadership, can influence the impact of professional development on teachers. Teachers who work in balanced, collaborative schools – characterised by high levels of both co-operation and instructional leadership – report both greater participation in school-embedded professional development activities and greater impact of those activities on their teaching.

Thus, "effective" teacher professional development that has an impact on teachers' instructional practices are activities that take place in schools and allow teachers to work, over time, in collaborative groups, on problems of practice. These types of activities are most likely to occur in schools that are characterised by co-operation among teachers and strong instructional leadership.

Policy makers can encourage participation in more effective professional development by first addressing the culture of schools. Structures and processes that encourage teachers to co-operate, including providing time and opportunities for teachers to do so, are needed. School leaders should be encouraged to focus on instructional leadership.

With the right school conditions in place, policy makers can also increase the amount and variation of school-embedded professional development offerings. These activities may include teacher-initiated research projects, teacher networks, observation of colleagues, and mentoring and coaching. Teacher participation in non-school embedded professional development should be limited. By supporting the conditions and activities most associated with effective teacher professional development, policy makers can increase the likelihood that students are positively affected.

There is also emerging evidence that the emphasis of professional development activities matters as well. Professional development could be used as a way to enhance teacher motivation. Indeed, teacher motivation is related to teachers' willingness to take advantage of learning opportunities and to engage in professional development (e.g. Nitsche, et al., 2013; Thoonen et al., 2011).

But most important, research is beginning to show that teacher professional development that is designed to build teachers' motivation is more successful in encouraging teachers to use new instructional strategies (e.g. Tschannen-Moran and McMaster, 2009).

### Including teachers in decision making

Figure 2.6 summarises the extent to which schools provide collaborative working environments, according to teachers' reports. Teachers who reported that they are provided with opportunities to participate in decision making at school reported greater job satisfaction (in all TALIS-participating countries and economies) and a greater sense of self-efficacy (in most countries/economies). The relationship between job satisfaction and teacher participation in school decision making is particularly strong in all countries.

Figure 2.6

**School decisions and collaborative school culture**

*Percentage of lower secondary principals who "strongly disagree", "disagree", "agree" or "strongly agree" with the following statements about their school*

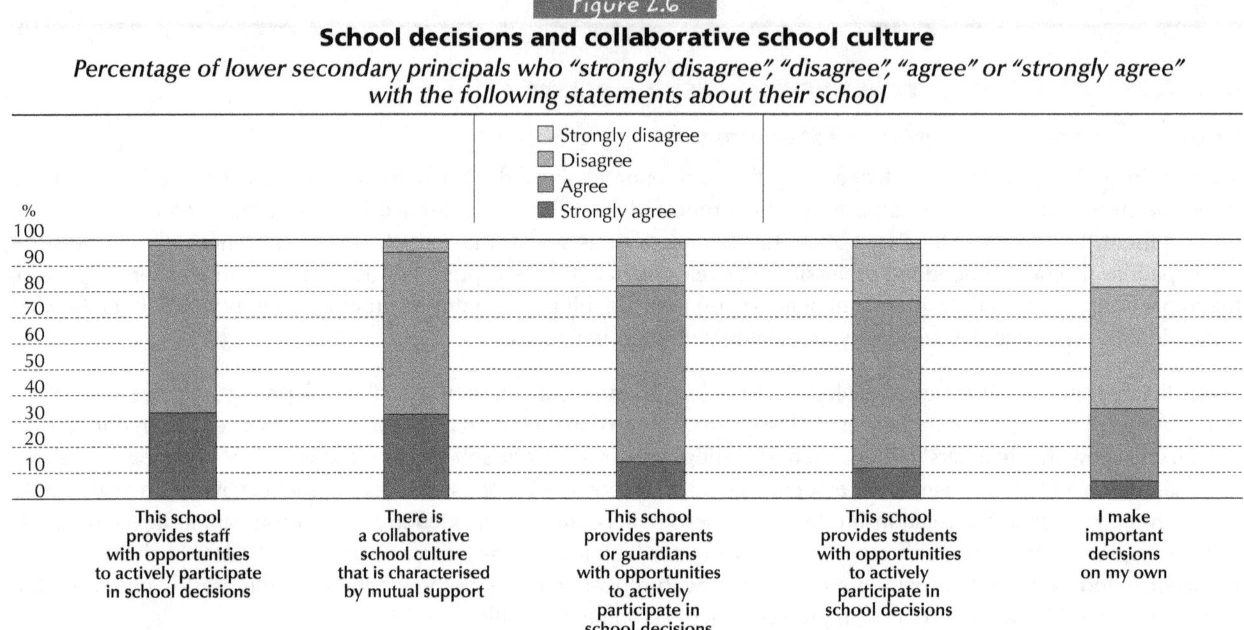


*Items are ranked in descending order of the percentage of principals who "agree" or "strongly agree" with the statement about their school.*
**Source:** OECD, TALIS 2013 Database, http://stats.oecd.org/index.aspx?datasetcode=talis_2013%20.
StatLink http://dx.doi.org/10.1787/888933330515

In addition, in almost all TALIS countries/economies, the extent to which teachers can participate in decision making has a strong positive association with the likelihood of reporting that teaching is a valued profession in society. Fewer than one in three teachers across TALIS countries/economies believe that teaching is a valued profession in society. But in all but one TALIS country, the extent to which teachers can participate in decision making has a strong, positive association with the likelihood of teachers reporting that teaching is valued profession in society.

The concept of distributed leadership is not only important for helping to alleviate some of the burden school leaders face, but it can be beneficial to teachers as well. Teachers are uniquely placed to aid in school-level decision making because they might be closer to students and parents, more familiar with how the curriculum is implemented, and better able to discuss student assessments and results than their school principals might be. Thus, it is not only worthwhile for school principals to devolve some of the responsibility for school-level decisions to teachers, but policy makers should consider providing guidance on distributed leadership and distributed decision making at the system level.

Figure 2.7 summarises the prevalence of practices for distributed leadership as reported by principals.

TALIS also shows that principals who participated in professional training or courses are more likely to create opportunities for staff, students and parents or guardians to take part in school decisions. There is a small, but significant, relationship between a principal's engagement in professional development activities and his or her distributional leadership. This concerns principals' participation in a professional network, mentoring or research activity, their participation in courses, conferences or observational visits, as well as principals' participation in other professional development activities.

Figure 2.7

**Distributed leadership in schools**

*Percentage of lower secondary principals who reported that they "often" or "very often" distributed leadership activities among other stakeholders in and around the school during the 12 months prior to the survey*

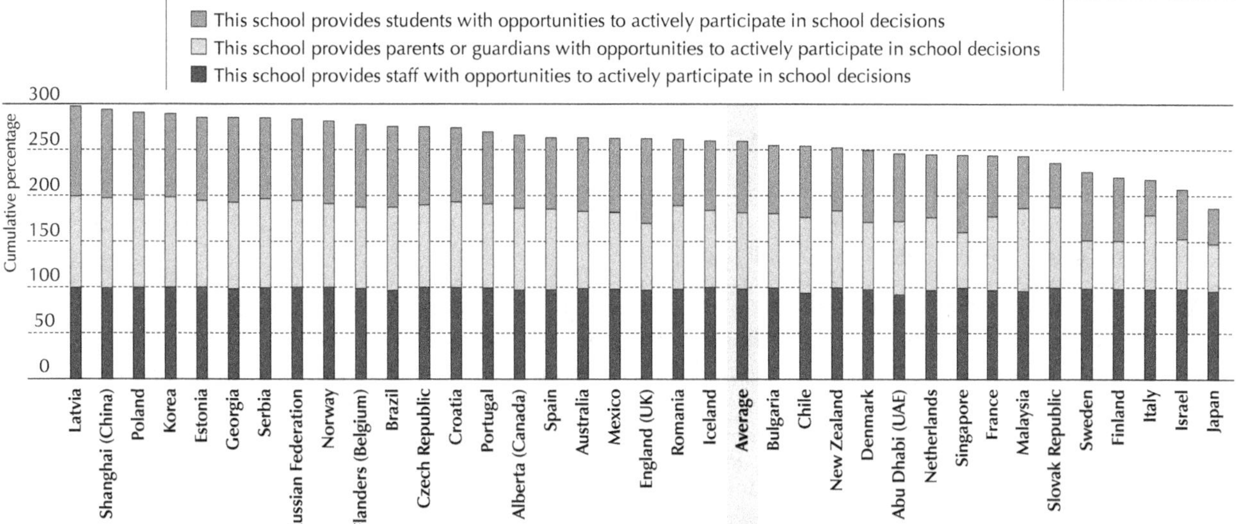


*Countries are ranked in descending order of the percentage of principals who reported that leadership activities are distributed among other stakeholders in their school.*

**Source:** OECD (2013), TALIS 2013 complete database, http://stats.oecd.org/index.aspx?datasetcode=talis_2013%20.

**StatLink** http://dx.doi.org/10.1787/888933330524

Distributed leadership is positively related to a shared sense of purpose in schools – one of the key components of professional learning communities. This finding, which is observed in primary, lower secondary and upper secondary education, suggests that involving students and their parents or guardians, in addition to school staff, creates a culture of shared responsibility for school issues, which is characterised by mutual support among all stakeholders. In lower secondary schools, a stronger emphasis on distributed leadership is also related to teachers who are more often involved in reflective dialogue and collaborative actions. However, these findings were not corroborated in primary and upper secondary education.

### Strengthening peer collaboration through induction programmes and mentoring

The first years of a teacher's career can make or break that career. Induction and support programmes for beginning teachers can improve the effectiveness and job satisfaction of new teachers – and thus make it less likely that those teachers will leave the profession at the first hurdle. The United States school districts of Cincinnati, Toledo and Rochester, for example, managed to reduce beginning teacher attrition by more than two-thirds by having expert mentors coach beginning teachers during their first year (National Commission on Teaching and America's Future, 1996). In addition, well-designed programmes help new teachers in applying the more theoretical knowledge acquired in their teacher-preparation programmes to teaching in the classroom. Well-developed induction programmes can give school systems a competitive edge in hiring new teachers.

The importance of induction programmes for new teachers in the early years of their teaching careers is now widely acknowledged. In successful programmes, mentor teachers provide guidance and supervision to beginning teachers in close collaboration with the initial teacher-education institution. These mentors provide on-the-job support, identify deficits in subject-matter knowledge, classroom management strategies and other pedagogical processes.

Central to the success of induction and mentoring programmes are the resources dedicated to those programmes and the quality of mentor training. Often, schools that would need to provide the most support to beginning teachers are the least capable of delivering high-quality induction programmes. Thus effective partnerships between teacher-education institutions and schools are particularly important.

TALIS defines induction programmes for teachers as a range of structured activities at school to introduce teachers to their new school (or into the teaching profession for new teachers). These activities could include peer work or mentoring (Box 2.3). Induction and mentoring programmes may help new teachers cope with initial difficulties and challenges.

Ingersoll and Strong (2011) reviewed empirical studies on the effects of support, guidance and orientation programmes (that is, induction programmes) for beginning teachers. They found that most of the studies provide empirical evidence for the claim that support and assistance for beginning teachers have a positive influence on several outcomes, such as teachers' commitment and retention, and student achievement. In particular, empirical evidence shows that students taught by teachers who had received comprehensive induction support show larger learning gains than those shown by students who are taught by teachers who had not received such support (see, for instance, Glazerman et al., 2010).

### Box 2.3 Induction programmes in Singapore and France

**The central role of induction in Singapore**

Upon completion of pre-service teacher education, beginning teachers in Singapore participate in induction programmes at both the national and school levels.

At the national level, they attend a three-day induction programme, called the Beginning Teachers' Orientation Programme, conducted by the Singapore Ministry of Education. This programme emphasises the importance of the role of teachers in nurturing the whole child and enables beginning teachers to consolidate their learning at the teacher institute. By presenting the roles and expectations of teachers, this programme also inducts new teachers into Singapore's teaching fraternity in the areas of professional beliefs, values and behaviours.

During the first two years of teaching, further guidance is provided to beginning teachers via the Structured Mentoring Programme. This programme enables teachers to learn practical knowledge and skills from assigned mentors who are experienced or senior teachers at the school. The school has the autonomy to customise the programme according to the learning needs of the new teachers. Besides practical skills, the programme helps to deepen the understanding of new teachers about the values and ethos of the teaching profession.

**Induction as part of a consecutive model of teacher education in France**

From the early 1990s to 2010, France had a consecutive model of teacher education. Training in academic subjects was largely predominant, which led to a high level of specialisation in secondary education teaching. After a bachelor's degree or higher, students sat a competitive examination for recruitment. Successful candidates received one year of training and were assigned a tutor. Since the early 2000s, new teachers have been mostly enrolled in formal induction programmes during their first year of regular employment, with scheduled time for activities. These specific programmes take place outside the schools, and are based on classroom practices to help new teachers manage a full-time job.

Launched in 2010, the reform called "mastérisation" made access to the teaching profession conditional upon completing a master's degree. A new structure of initial teacher education was elaborated under the education act of July 2013, and has been in effect since the start of the 2013/14 school year. Within graduate schools of professorship and education (*Écoles supérieures du Professorat et de l'Enseignement,* ESPE), which are integral parts of the universities, the study programmes combine academic subject studies, theoretical pedagogy and practical teaching experience to ensure a progressive start to the teaching profession. Induction programmes still exist, but they are now reduced and included in other in-service teacher training activities. If available, they are often focused on classroom management in order to respond to new teachers' needs, especially those assigned to difficult areas.

**Sources:** Ministry of Education, Singapore; Ministry of Education, France.

As shown in Figure 2.8, whereas, on average, 70% of these less-experienced teachers work in schools whose principals reported that induction programmes are available, only slightly more than half of these teachers reported having taken part in such programmes. This means that some teachers who have access to such programmes may not be taking advantage of them.

Another element of professional development is mentoring, which TALIS defines as a support structure in schools where more-experienced teachers support less-experienced teachers. This structure might involve all teachers in the school or only new teachers. The literature similarly defines mentoring as personal guidance, usually provided by more-experienced teachers to beginning teachers. The overall objective of teacher-mentoring programmes is to give newcomers a local guide; but the character and content of these programmes varies widely. In addition, evidence shows that the students of teachers who receive more hours of mentoring achieve at higher levels than those whose teachers had fewer hours of mentoring (Rockoff, 2008).

Figure 2.8

**Formal induction for new teachers**

*Percentage of lower secondary teachers who have less than three years of experience at their school and less than three years of experience as a teacher who are working in schools where the principal reported access to formal induction programmes, and the percentage of teachers with the same characteristics who reported having participated in formal induction programmes*[1, 2]

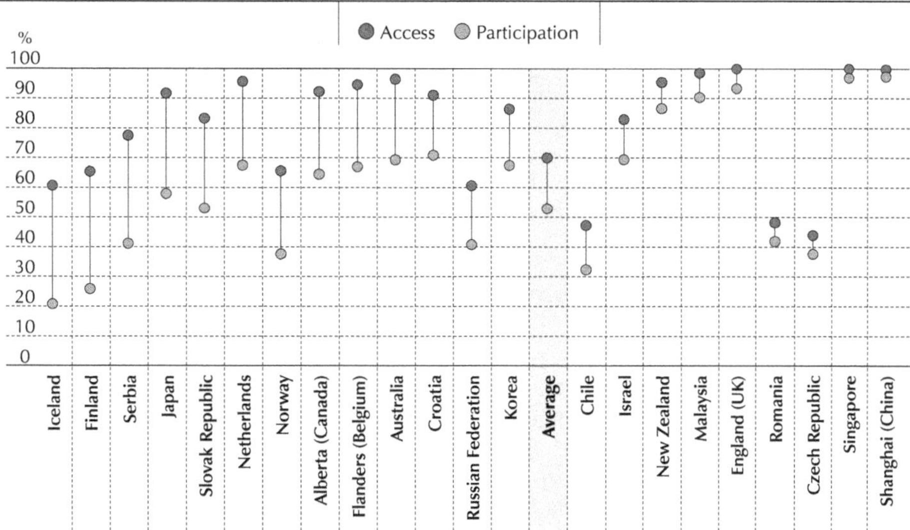


1. Data on access to induction programmes are derived from the principal questionnaire, while data on participation are derived from the teacher questionnaire. Teachers were asked about their participation in an induction programme in their first regular employment as a teacher.

2. Data presented in this figure are for formal induction programmes only, meaning they do not consider participation in or access to informal induction activities as part of an induction programme or a general and/or administrative introduction to the school.

*Countries are ranked in descending order of the gap between access to and participation in induction programmes. Countries are not presented in this graph if the percentage of teachers with less than three years of experience at their school and less than three years of experience as a teacher is below 5%.*

**Source:** OECD (2013), TALIS 2013 complete database, http://stats.oecd.org/index.aspx?datasetcode=talis_2013%20.

StatLink http://dx.doi.org/10.1787/888933330535

The proportion of teachers who work in schools whose principal reported that mentoring programmes are available for all teachers is larger than the proportion of teachers who reported that they have a mentor. This suggests that not all teachers in schools with mentoring programmes for all teachers report having mentors. In some countries, however, there is a large difference between the proportion of teachers who work in schools with mentoring programmes for all teachers and the proportion of teachers who report having a mentor. School leaders need to highlight the benefits of such programmes for teachers and remove any barriers to access to ensure that teachers can participate in these activities and reap the benefits that ensue.

There are different ways in which participation in induction and mentoring programmes can be beneficial. Empirical evidence shows that students taught by teachers who receive comprehensive induction support achieve at a higher level than students taught by teachers who did not receive such support (Glazerman et al., 2010).

There is also evidence of a positive association between induction/mentoring participation and teacher self-efficacy. In 14 of the countries/economies that participated in TALIS, teachers who reported that they had participated in a formal induction programme have higher levels of self-efficacy. New teachers seem to benefit most from mentoring. For them, time spent with a mentor, participation in mentor-facilitated professional development activities, and the quality of mentors' interactions are significantly related to the teachers' self-efficacy and the development of collaborative relationships with their colleagues (LoCasale-Crouch et al., 2012).

There is a similar, positive association between participation in induction programmes in the past, and in collaborative practices and professional development later in the career, suggesting a long-term impact of induction processes.

Teachers' past participation in induction programmes improves their performance and thus might better prepare them to serve as mentors. TALIS examined the effect of having participated in induction activities in the past on the likelihood of a teacher acting as mentor in the present. The results show that in 17 countries, teachers who reported that they had participated in a formal induction programme in the past were more likely to report that they currently act as a mentor than

those who reported that they had not participated in such programmes (in the remainder of the countries, this relationship is not statistically significant). These results suggest that early policy interventions, such as, for example, participating in an induction programme during the first job, might have a long-term impact on teachers' later willingness to help other teachers to improve their teaching capacities. Box 2.4 describes an induction programme with a mentoring component in Ontario, Canada.

### Box 2.4 New Teacher Induction Program in Ontario, Canada

The New Teacher Induction Program (NTIP) is seen as a step in a continuum of professional learning for teachers to support effective teaching, learning and assessment practices. It provides an additional full year of professional support so that new teachers can continue to develop the skills and knowledge needed to be effective in their work.

The NTIP consists of the following induction elements:

- orientation for all new teachers to the school and school board
- mentoring for new teachers by experienced teachers
- professional development and training.

New teachers are defined as those certified by the Ontario College of Teachers who have been hired into permanent positions – full-time or part-time – by a school board, school authority or provincial school to begin teaching for the first time in Ontario.

To successfully complete the NTIP, new teachers must achieve two satisfactory ratings on teacher performance appraisals for new teachers. New teachers who successfully complete two performance appraisals within the required time will receive a notation of successful completion of the NTIP on their Certificate of Qualification and Registration and on the OCT public register.

**Source:** Ministry of Education, Ontario, Canada.

Figure 2.9

### Predicted effect of participation in a formal induction programme on participation in professional development

*Probability of participation in three or more professional development activities for lower secondary teachers who reported having participated in a formal induction programme versus teachers who reported that they had not participated in such programmes[1]*

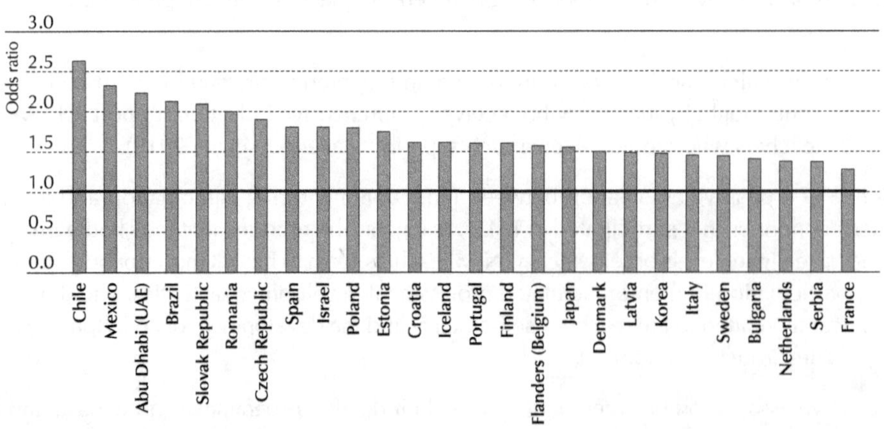


1. Countries for which the odds ratio is not statistically significant at 5% or where data represent less than 5% of the cases are not presented in this figure.

**Note:** The analysis was run only for the countries that participated in TALIS 2013 in 2012-13. Thus, Georgia, New Zealand, the Russian Federation and Shanghai (China) are not included in the figure.

*Countries are ranked in descending order of the predicted effect of having participated in an induction programme on the reported number of professional development activities.*

**Source:** OECD, TALIS 2013 Database, http://stats.oecd.org/index.aspx?datasetcode=talis_2013%20.

StatLink http://dx.doi.org/10.1787/888933330541

Similarly, Figure 2.9 shows, at the country level, the predicted effect of teachers' past participation in induction programmes on the probability of their reporting that they had participated in three or more different types of professional development activities over the preceding 12 months. Although the results should be interpreted with caution, the significant positive relationships shown in the figure could indicate that promoting induction programmes might encourage teachers' future participation in professional development activities. Being involved in induction activities might spark teachers' interest in remaining up-to-date in content and pedagogical knowledge by taking advantage of further learning opportunities.

### *Building a collaborative school culture*

Formal collaborative learning generally entails teachers meeting on a regular basis to develop shared responsibility for their students' and school's success (Chong and Kong, 2012). A collaborative culture can be created and nurtured in many ways (Boxes 2.5 and 2.6). Empirical evidence shows that collaboration among teachers may enhance teacher efficacy, which, in turn, may improve student achievement and sustain positive teacher behaviours (Liaw, 2009; Puchner and Taylor, 2006). In a meta-review of empirical studies, Cordingley et al. (2015) reported that collaborative professional development is related to a positive impact on teachers' range of teaching practices and instruction strategies, to their ability to match these to their students' needs, and to their self-esteem and self-efficacy. There is also evidence that such collaborative professional development is linked to a positive influence on student learning processes, motivation and outcomes.

Results from TALIS show that collaborative practices are related to both higher levels of self-efficacy and job satisfaction. In particular, teachers who reported that they participate in collaborative professional learning five times a year or more also reported significantly greater self-efficacy in almost all countries (Figure 2.10) and higher job satisfaction in two out of three countries. The practice most strongly related to teachers' self-efficacy is taking part in collaborative professional learning. In almost all countries, teachers who engage in this activity five times a year or more also show higher levels of self-efficacy; in half of the countries, this relationship is moderately strong.

Figure 2.10

**Teachers' self-efficacy and professional collaboration**

*Lower secondary teachers' self-efficacy level according to the frequency of professional collaboration*

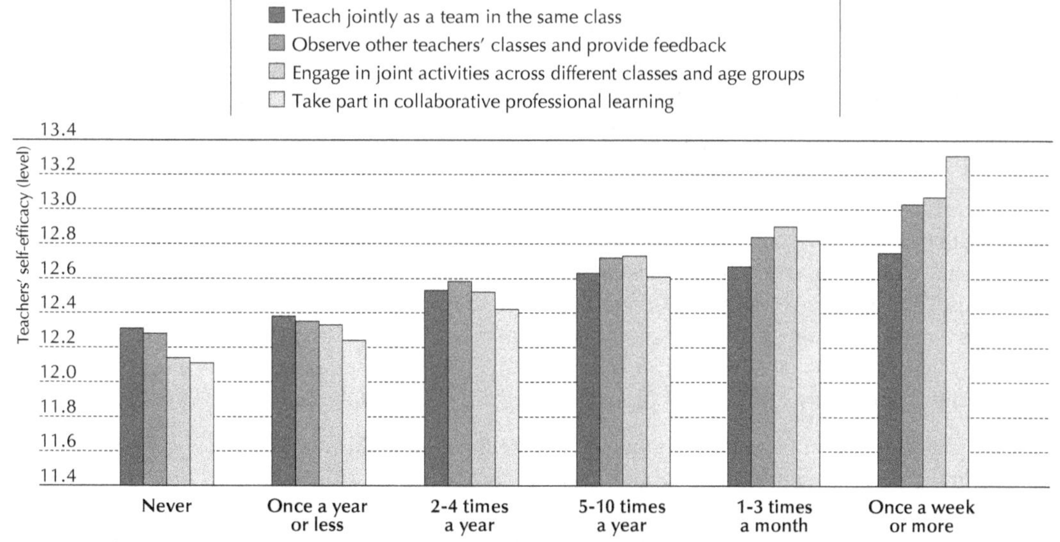


Source: OECD (2013), TALIS 2013 complete database, http://stats.oecd.org/index.aspx?datasetcode=talis_2013%20.
StatLink http://dx.doi.org/10.1787/888933330558

Many of the collaborative practices discussed in TALIS, such as observing other teachers' classes and providing feedback or teaching as a team in the same class, could – and should – be performed at the school level. These activities serve a variety of purposes, such as providing professional development for teachers in the context within which they work or offering teachers another source of feedback on their work. School leaders need to make teachers' schedules more flexible to allow for such practices as team teaching. The benefits of doing so are likely to outweigh any logistical burden.

TALIS data also show that challenging classroom circumstances can affect teachers' self-efficacy and job satisfaction. While class size does not show any relationship to either self-efficacy or job satisfaction, certain classroom characteristics can make a teacher's work more challenging. Teachers teaching classes where more than one in ten students are low academic achievers or have behavioural problems show significantly lower self-efficacy (in 9 and 16 of the TALIS countries/economies, respectively). At the same time, TALIS results show that the interpersonal relationships in a school have powerful mediating effects on some of the challenging classroom circumstances that teachers might face. Positive interpersonal relationships can mitigate the otherwise detrimental effects that challenging classrooms might have on a teacher's job satisfaction or feelings of self-efficacy. In addition, teachers' active engagement in research can also enhance practice in the classroom (Box 2.6) and non-governmental organisations can play an important role too (Box 2.7).

### Box 2.5 Building collaborative networks within schools in the Netherlands

Aiming to improve the teaching profession and promote the excellence of education, the Netherlands recently introduced a comprehensive strategy called the Teachers' Programme (*Lerarenagenda 2013-2020*). The main aims of the programme are:

- attracting high-performing students into teacher training programmes
- improving teacher pre-service training programmes
- providing attractive and flexible development pathways
- developing support for teachers at the start of their careers
- developing schools as learning organisations by engaging teachers, school leaders and school boards
- helping all teachers maintain and develop their skills and qualifications
- sustaining a strong professional organisation that represents teachers.

**Source:** OECD (2014).

### Box 2.6 The HertsCam M.Ed in Leading Teaching and Learning

The HertsCam M.Ed, a two-year master's degree programme for serving teachers and other practitioners in education, is distinctive in that it is entirely taught by practitioners currently serving as teachers in secondary and primary schools in Hertsfordshire, England. These "scholar practitioners" are all graduates of the programme and some are engaged in part-time doctoral study. All have been involved in research and development both locally and internationally and have published, thus as teachers in the programme, they can draw on both their everyday professional experience and their academic knowledge.

The programme is based on the concept of "teacher-led development work" which aims to mobilise teachers and other education practitioners as agents of change regardless of their status or position. In HertsCam, development work is defined as strategic, focused, planned and deliberate attempts to improve an aspect of professional practice through incremental steps. This largely involves analysis, data collection, reflection and deliberation in collaborative contexts. A range of experiences, tools and academic resources are used to enable participants to analyse their institutional contexts, identify their professional concerns, and consult with colleagues and stakeholders to create an agenda for change. Participants then design development projects through which they take action to address their concerns.

The programme rests on seven pedagogic foundations: activities that cultivate moral purpose; participants lead development projects; communities in which critical friendship can flourish; reflection on experience through dialogue; the art of critical narrative writing through which scholarship illuminates problem solving; the use of conceptual tools that deepen understanding of how to develop practice; and professional knowledge built through local and international networking. The programme is implemented mostly in school classrooms at the end of the school day with a two-day residential conference held in a hotel each term.

The programme began with its first cohort of participants from primary and secondary schools in September 2015. HertsCam aspires to develop this as an international programme in collaboration with NGOs and other relevant organisations around the world.

**Source:** Frost, D. (2015).

### Box 2.7 Charitable foundations as partners in the professionalisation of teachers

Since the 1990s, not-for-profit foundations have become increasingly involved in the education sector in Germany. In the past few years, various foundations have become active in promoting and rewarding innovative teachers. For example:

- The Vodafone Foundation Germany honours outstanding teachers each year with the "German Teacher's Award". Teachers are nominated for the award by their pupils.
- The not-for-profit Hertie Foundation offers a scholarship programme for students with an immigrant background who want to become teachers.
- The "German School Academy" of the Robert Bosch Foundation offers teachers and school leaders information on creating excellent schools based on the profiles of schools that have been honoured with the "German School Award".
- The *Stiftung der Deutschen Wirtschaft* (German Economy Foundation) aims to promote skills development for school leaders and introduce new leadership and management concepts into teacher training through its "Leadership in Teacher Training" programme.
- The aim of the *Deutsche Telekom Stiftung* (German Telecom Foundation) is to support education, science and research in the STEM subjects. It promotes enhancement of teacher training in STEM subjects at partner universities.

Not-for-profit foundations are granted tax concessions by the state. Although foundations do not assume any sovereign tasks in the education sector, they are important initiators and multipliers of innovations in education policy, including in teacher training, and are regarded as such by federal government, *Länder* and local authorities.

**Source:** Standing Conference of the Ministers of Education and Cultural Affairs of the *Länder* in the Federal Republic of Germany.

### *Supporting a culture of student assessment*

Organising professional development activities about student assessment is common practice in many countries. Gilmore (2008) makes a distinction between professional development programmes in which assessment is "foregrounded" (i.e. it is the main focus of the programme) and those programmes where assessment is "backgrounded", (i.e. the programme does not focus on assessment, per se, but assessment is an integral part of the programme). Many countries use a mix of both.

In Australia, most jurisdictions provide training to improve the competency of teachers to analyse and interpret student-assessment data. For example, the Victorian Curriculum and Assessment Authority conducts in-service courses in schools around Victoria to develop school leaders' and teachers' skills in interpreting the results of the national assessments and the Victorian Certificate of Education exam (Santiago et al., 2011). In the Flemish Community of Belgium, courses on assessment are an important part of the wide range of in-service training possibilities. It is common practice for schools to invite experts on various items (e.g. student assessment) to provide training opportunities for teachers (Flemish Ministry of Education and Training, 2010). In the French Community of Belgium, professional development on assessment is also available. The subjects addressed in in-service training courses are determined based on needs identified by the *Commission de pilotage* and the Inspectorate (Blondin and Giot, 2011). In Korea, in-service training on assessment is provided as part of the national training framework. In recent years, local education offices and individual schools have also been adding new dimensions to the contents and methodology of such training (Kim et al., 2010).

New Zealand's Ministry of Education has initiated several major professional development programmes that have been evaluated in terms of their impact on student learning, with promising results (Nusche et al., 2012). For example, "Assess to Learn" (AtoL) is a whole-school professional development programme that has been offered to primary and secondary schools since 2002. Schools apply to participate in the programme and typically participate for two years. The annual budget for AtoL is NZD 3.17 million and the programme currently involves 155 schools. The programme aims to support teachers in choosing adequate assessment tools and analysing assessment information so as to advance student learning. A 2008 evaluation of the AtoL programme reported that the programme had significant impact on teachers' professional practice and student performance, especially among students with initially low levels of achievement. Monitoring data showed that schools participating in AtoL had achieved up to 4.5 times greater improvements in writing in grades 4 to 9 than the national expected rate of progress.

In some countries, the focus on professional development for student assessment has been considerably reinforced in recent years. In Hungary, for example, awareness-raising campaigns on assessment were held in every region in 2009. These occasions can also serve to strengthen the reputation and acceptance of assessments, and give professional impetus to make the use of the results. In Mexico, teachers are being offered a greater number of assessment-related training opportunities. Most of the programmes are targeted at school supervisors and focus on competencies-based assessment. Many subject-specific courses include new approaches, techniques and instruments for classroom-based assessment (Santiago et al., 2012). In Norway, student assessment is also highlighted as a key topic in continuing professional development. Since 2005, the Directorate for Education and Training has included student assessment as one of the annual priorities for continuing professional development of teachers, school leaders and trainers of in-service training providers (Nusche et al., 2011).

Professional development can also take place through moderation of teachers' assessment and marking. Moderation refers to quality-assurance measures that seek to increase the consistency of marking by, for example, having teachers within or across schools review or cross-mark each other's assessments or work together in groups to discuss assessment criteria and student performance. Moderation is a key strategy in validating the consistency of teachers' judgements and marking. At the same time, moderation also involves professional discussions among teachers about the quality of student work. As such, it is a professional learning opportunity that is closely related to their classroom practices. It also helps to improve teachers' professional judgements about student work and helps them to develop a shared understanding of marking criteria or standards within and among schools (Timperley et al., 2008).

Professional learning may also provide opportunities for teachers and schools to network with each other or with assessment advisors and disseminate effective practice. In Norway, the Better Assessment Practices project (2007-09) supported a range of local projects to improve assessment practice in Norwegian schools. As a follow-up, the Assessment for Learning programme (2010-14) was implemented to support school projects and networks focusing on formative assessment. There are also local initiatives in this area. The City of Oslo, for example, employs two "assessment advisors" whom schools can invite to provide help regarding assessments (Nusche et al., 2011). In Denmark, resource teachers in schools support teachers. Although there are few assessment and evaluation advisors (only 8% of schools reported having these), they can offer critical support to teachers whose initial training did not emphasise student assessment and evaluation (Shewbridge et al., 2011). In Canada, all school boards have created assessment divisions or sectors within their administrative structure and have assigned personnel to lead workshops, develop activities related to assessments, and track, collate, analyse and distribute findings of district-wide assessments to their respective stakeholders (Fournier and Mildon, forthcoming).

However, while there are professional development opportunities in the area of student assessment in most countries, there is often little information available at the central level about the extent to which teachers benefit from them and about the quality of courses available. In education systems where schools and teachers are free to determine the content of their professional development courses, it is often unclear to what extent teachers choose to improve their student-assessment methods through such courses.

### *Strengthening links between teacher appraisal and professional development*

Teacher appraisal, part and parcel of effective teacher policies, will deliver best results if it is linked to professional development. In order for a vibrant programme of professional development to be established and sustained, it must be based on a culture of professional inquiry and on the professional obligation of every teacher to be engaged in a career-long quest to improve practice.

A key objective of teacher appraisal is to identify areas for professional development for individual teachers, leading to the preparation of individual improvement plans that take into account the school's development plan. Pedagogical leadership at the school level plays a key role in ensuring the effectiveness of this link (Pont et al., 2008).

Information collected from countries participating in the OECD Reviews on Assessment and Evaluation in Education (OECD, 2013b) indicates that all types of teacher appraisal, except explicit reward schemes, may influence future professional development activities (Table 2.2). Regular teacher appraisal as part of performance management is most typically associated with professional development activities or plans. It systematically influences professional development in Australia, Korea, Mexico and Northern Ireland (United Kingdom) and it is expected/intended to do so in Austria, the Flemish Community of Belgium, some provinces/territories in Canada, France, Israel, the Netherlands, New Zealand and Slovenia.

The Teacher Performance Appraisal system in the Canadian province of Ontario, for example, has two components: one for "new" teachers and one for "experienced" teachers. Experienced teachers undergo a comprehensive performance appraisal, conducted by the principal, and are evaluated according to 16 competencies that define the skills, knowledge and attitudes of effective teaching. Experienced teachers are appraised once every five years. In addition, they set goals for continuous learning and improvement through the completion of an Annual Learning Plan each year. Appraisals of new teachers focus on eight of the 16 competencies. New teachers must be appraised at least twice in the first 12 months of teaching. New teachers who receive two satisfactory ratings during their new teaching period receive a notation on their Certificate of Qualification from the Ontario College of Teachers (Ministry of Education, Ontario, Canada).

In Chile, teacher appraisal systematically results in a professional development plan for teachers who have obtained a "basic" or "poor" rating; in Portugal, this is the case for teachers who have obtained an "insufficient" rating. In the Czech Republic, Hungary, Poland and the Slovak Republic, the link between regular appraisal for performance management and professional development is not prescribed nationally, but it may well exist at the school level. Practices vary across schools, depending on internal regulations.

Table 2.2

**Influence of teacher appraisal on professional development (2011-12)**

*Percentage of lower secondary principals who reported having received leadership training in their formal education[1]*

| | | Performance management | | |
|---|---|---|---|---|
| | Completion of probation | Regular appraisal | Registration | Promotion |
| **It systematically influences professional development activities** | Northern Ireland (UK) | Australia, Chile,[2] Korea, Mexico, Portugal,[2] Northern Ireland (UK) | Australia | Czech Republic[3] |
| **It is expected/intended to influence professional development activities** | Australia, Canada, Ireland, Israel, Netherlands, New Zealand | Austria, Flanders (Belgium), Canada, France, Israel, Netherlands, New Zealand, Slovenia | New Zealand | Israel |
| **It may influence professional development activities, depending on school policies and practices** | Slovak Republic | Czech Republic, Hungary, Poland, Slovak Republic | -- | -- |
| **It does not influence teacher professional development** | France,[1] Italy, Luxembourg, Slovenia | -- | Sweden | Estonia, Korea, Poland |

1. France: But a negative appraisal may result in a second year of *stage*.
2. Chile, Portugal: It systematically results in a professional development plan for teachers who have obtained a low rating only.
3. Czech Republic: It influences professional development if connected with promotion to particular professional status.
**Note:** Derived from information supplied by countries participating in the project. The table should be interpreted as providing broad indications only, and not strict comparability across countries.
**Source:** OECD (2013), *Synergies for Better Learning: An International Perspective on Evaluation and Assessment*, http://dx.doi.org/10.1787/9789264190658-en.

Appraisal at completion of probation also influences professional development in Northern Ireland (United Kingdom), and it is expected to do so in Australia, some provinces/territories in Canada, Ireland, Israel, the Netherlands and New Zealand. Registration systematically influences professional development in Australia and is expected to do so in New Zealand. The promotion scheme in Israel is also expected to inform future professional development. In the Czech Republic, appraisal for promotion influences professional development if it is related to accession to a particular professional status, such as that of pedagogical advisor.

A link between performance appraisal and continuing professional development opportunities is essential to improve teaching practice (Ofsted, 2006). Identifying individual teachers' strengths and weaknesses is crucial for choosing from among a wide range of possible professional development activities those that meet individual teachers' own needs against each of the priorities in the school-improvement plan. It is important that teachers regard appraisal as the first step towards improved practice, regardless of their current level of performance.

However, among the teachers participating in TALIS, over 40% reported that they did not receive suggestions for improving aspects of their work; 44% agreed with the statement that teachers' work was reviewed merely to fulfil an administrative requirement. Also, according to principals' reports, only 56.6% of teachers were in schools where the identification of a specific weakness in a teacher's practice always or most of the time leads to establishing a professional development plan for the teacher.

These are worrying results. Without a clear link to professional growth opportunities, the impact of teacher appraisal on teaching and learning will be relatively limited. As a result, the appraisal process may not be taken seriously or may be treated with mistrust or indifference by the teachers being appraised. Ideally, teacher appraisal should allow teachers to receive tailored feedback, and such feedback should be followed with opportunities for continuous learning.

Teachers' learning should also be thought of as something broader than participation in in-service training courses. According to Timperley (2011), the term "professional development" is now often associated with the delivery of some kind of information to teachers in order to influence their practice. By contrast, "professional learning" refers to a more internal process through which teachers create professional knowledge by interacting with this information in a way that challenges previous assumptions and creates new meanings. Such professional learning cultures need to be supported and sustained by effective pedagogical leadership. All teachers, including those who are highly effective, need opportunities to learn and grow in the teaching profession. Box 2.8 provides examples of how appraisal results are used for professional development in Korea and in Memphis, Tennessee, in the United States. Box 2.9 highlights ways to involve teachers in this process.

### Box 2.8 Linking teacher appraisal to professional development

In **Korea**'s Teacher Appraisal for Professional Development programme, once appraisal procedures are completed, evaluation sheets are collected and drafted into a final report for each teacher. Results of the peer-review process are written up by "appraisal-management committees" at each school. Upon receiving their appraisal results report, teachers prepare their own plans for professional development (including plans to attend training) and submit these to the appraisal-management committee. The committee brings together the professional development plans and the appraisal results of all appraised teachers, and drafts a "synthetic report on Teacher Appraisal for Professional Development" to submit to the principal and vice principal. The synthetic report must include: implementation plan and progress of appraisal; overall appraisal results (excluding results for individual teachers); general features of appraisal (appraisal provided by parents, students and peer teachers; strengths and weaknesses of the school's teachers as revealed by appraisal); teachers' demand for training, including autonomous in-service training; fields of training requested by the teachers; the school's next-year plans to provide consulting and training programmes for teachers' professional development; budget estimation; and proposals and requests to the local education authority (demands for the establishment of new training programmes, requests for budget support for in-service training by the education office, etc.).

Based on the appraisal results, local education authorities provide excellent teachers with a "study and research year" (similar to sabbatical years given to university faculty) as a way of granting opportunities for teachers to build their professional capacity. Underperforming teachers are obliged to participate in short- to long-term training programmes, depending on their appraisal results. Regardless of appraisal outcomes, local education offices support teachers with customised training programmes so as to foster an atmosphere of self-study and self-improvement among teachers. Individual appraisal reports are shared only with the concerned teacher and principal. Only the average results of all teachers appraised in a school are disseminated among parents and students.

The city of **Memphis** in **Tennessee (United States)** has developed a system that explicitly links professional learning to teacher appraisal. In Memphis city schools, appraisal is based on teaching standards, and professional development is linked to teachers' competence measured against those standards. Thus, a teacher who shows poor performance on a specific indicator of a teaching standard can find professional growth opportunities related to that indicator. Memphis city schools publish a professional development guide each year that lists the professional growth offerings by standard and indicator. In addition, most of the professional development courses are taught by Memphis city school teachers, ensuring that the course offerings will be relevant to the contexts in which these teachers work.

**Sources:** Kim et al. (2010); Memphis City Schools, www.mcsk12.net; Santiago et al. (2013).

Teacher appraisal and feedback can be used to recognise and celebrate teachers' strengths while simultaneously challenging teachers to address weaknesses in their pedagogical practices. Appraisal and feedback can have a significant impact on classroom instruction, teacher motivation and attitudes, as well as on student outcomes. Specifically, appraisal and feedback can play an important role in teachers' job satisfaction and self-efficacy. Whereas teachers say they derive little value from student ratings, teacher-solicited feedback is generally regarded as the most useful source of information for improving teaching (Wininger and Birkholz, 2013; Ross and Bruce, 2007; Michaelowa, 2002).

### Box 2.9 Involving teachers in creating a culture of evaluation

Involving teachers in school policies and practices is an essential component of modern education governance. This is especially important in practices and policies around evaluation and assessment, both in building a culture of evaluation in the system and in incorporating a broader perspective in decisions about what does and does not work. Yet devising the policies is just the first step; implementation and ownership by teachers are critical to their success.

**Poland**, for example, introduced a new school-supervision process in 2009 in which practitioners were more directly involved in the evaluation process. This supervision system reinforced collaboration and self-assessment among educators, and changed the role of school inspectors and chief inspectors. Key elements of success included providing comprehensive information to the teachers as well as to school leaders and inspectors. This involved clearly defining goals, steps to achieve the goals and development plans. Interestingly, it was the schools that had some familiarity with restructuring – for example, some schools had previously implemented an inter-school quality-assurance system that involved the entire school community – that were initially most receptive to the reform. In these schools, a significant part of the teaching staff eagerly participated in trainings provided by the new school-supervision system.

Similarly, **Norway**'s implementation of the Assessment for Learning (AfL) programme aimed to motivate authorities, schools and training establishments to develop a culture of assessment with a strong focus on learning. Not surprisingly, the municipalities that most successfully implemented the programme demonstrated clear communication between governance levels and a high degree of trust among stakeholders. On the local level, the establishment of learning networks among schools aided the exchange of knowledge and provided peer support during the implementation. Integrating teachers in the change process (e.g. by organising pre-planned visits to classrooms), and a willingness to adapt the implementation strategy to local contexts greatly facilitated the implementation and acceptance of the programme in schools.

These examples show some of the common elements required for successful policy implementation: communication, collaboration, and a willingness to take part in the change process. Establishing a set of shared priorities is also important, especially for smaller municipalities or schools that might feel overwhelmed by a number of different reforms and policy priorities that are taking place at the same time. However, building a culture of evaluation has its own specific challenges. One of the biggest initial barriers is a lack of trust: trust in what is being communicated, and also trust that evaluation could be used for improvement rather than punitively. The most successful systems work on all of the elements together, to steer the system, build trust, and use the strength and expertise of their schools and teachers to make reform happen.

**Sources:** Mazurkiewicz et al. (2014); Hopfenbeck et al. (2013).

## LEADING CHANGE FROM THE CLASSROOM

### *Linking professional autonomy with a collaborative culture*

PISA 2012 asked school principals to report how frequently various actions and behaviours related to managing their school, including teacher participation in school management, occurred in the previous academic year. On average across OECD countries, 72% of students are in schools whose principals reported that the school gives staff opportunities to make decisions concerning the school at least once a month; 54% are in schools that give these opportunities from once a month to once a week; and 18% are in schools that give these opportunities more than once a week. Over 80% of students in Australia, Brazil, Canada, Chile, Colombia, Denmark, Finland, Germany, Iceland, Jordan, New Zealand, Norway, Portugal, Sweden, Thailand, Turkey and the United States attend schools that give staff these opportunities at least once a month; while in France, Liechtenstein, Luxembourg, Macao (China), Poland, Romania and Shanghai (China), less than 50% of students attend such schools.

Across OECD countries, an average of 70% of students are in schools whose principal reported that teachers are involved at least once a month in building a culture of continuous improvement in the school; 47% of students are in schools where this occurs once a month to once a week; and 23% are in schools where this occurs more than once a week. Over 80% of students in Australia, Brazil, Canada, Chile, Denmark, Germany, Indonesia, Jordan, Latvia, Liechtenstein, Malaysia,

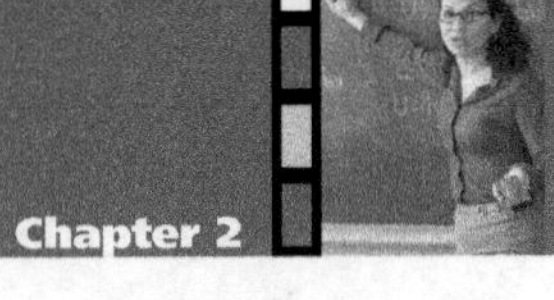



New Zealand, Portugal, Singapore, Slovenia, Sweden, Thailand, Turkey, the United Arab Emirates, the United Kingdom, the United States and Uruguay attend schools where teachers are involved in this activity at least once a month; while in France, Japan, Luxembourg, Macao (China), Romania and Shanghai (China), less than 50% of students attend such schools.

On average across OECD countries, 29% of students are in schools whose principal reported that teachers are asked to review management practices at least once a month; 24% are in schools where teachers do so once a month to once a week; and 6% are in schools where teachers do so more than once a week. Over 50% of students in Albania, Australia, Brazil, Bulgaria, Indonesia, Jordan, Kazakhstan, Korea, Malaysia, Montenegro, Thailand, Turkey, the United Arab Emirates, the United Kingdom and the United States attend schools where teachers participate in this activity at least once a month; while in France, Hungary, Luxembourg, Shanghai (China) and Switzerland, around 10% or less of students attend such schools.

Results from PISA suggest that the relationship between school autonomy and student performance is affected by whether there is a culture of collaboration between teachers and principals in managing the school. The results show that, in school systems where principals reported less teacher participation in school management (i.e. 1.5 index points lower on the PISA *index of teacher participation* than the OECD average), even after students' and schools' socio-economic status and demographic profile are taken into account, a student who attends a school with greater autonomy in allocating resources tends to score 17 points lower in mathematics than a student who attends a school with less autonomy. In contrast, in school systems where principals reported more teacher participation in school management (i.e. 1.5 index points higher than the OECD average), a student who attends a school with greater autonomy scores 9 points higher in mathematics than a student who attends a school with less autonomy. In short, school autonomy combined with a culture of participatory leadership tends to be associated with better learning outcomes.

### *Involving teachers in developing professional standards*

Another way to draw on the expertise in the classroom to build professional knowledge is to involve teachers in the development of professional standards. Indeed, for teaching standards to be relevant and owned by the profession, it is essential that teachers play a lead role in developing and taking responsibility for them. The participation of teachers in designing standards and procedures for teacher appraisal is essential to the effectiveness of any appraisal system. Inviting teachers to participate is a way of recognising their professionalism, the importance of their skills and experience, and the extent of their responsibilities. Teachers will be more open to being appraised if they are consulted in the process. Thus appraisal-system designers need to work with teachers' unions, teacher professional organisations and outstanding teachers from across the system. Australia and New Zealand provide some examples of this (Box 2.10).

#### Box 2.10 Involving the teaching profession in developing professional standards

In **Australia**, up until 2012 there were two types of teaching standards. First, each jurisdiction's statutory teaching body developed its own set of teaching standards to register teachers and accredit initial teacher-education programmes. Second, a number of education authorities also developed distinct professional standards for teachers (e.g. South Australia, Victoria, Western Australia) which generally provided the reference for performance-management processes and established links to the career structure. One of the system's strengths lies in the extensive involvement of the teaching profession, employers and teacher educators in developing teaching standards for registration/accreditation. Teaching colleges/institutes as independent statutory bodies provide teachers with professional autonomy and self-regulation and the right to have a say in the development of their profession. This reinforces the use of standards as a lever for improving teaching practices. In this context, a particularly significant development was the creation of the Australian Institute for Teaching and School Leadership (AITSL), whose aim is to establish a nationally shared understanding of what counts as accomplished teaching and school leadership. A significant achievement since the Institute was created in 2010 was the development of the Australian Professional Standards for Teachers (formerly known as the National Professional Standards for Teachers), which provides a national measure for teaching practice. The standards were developed in close consultation with the teaching profession, employers and teachers' educators, and are implemented across the country.

The **New Zealand** Teaching Council (NZTC) has developed teaching standards for registering teachers (the Registered Teacher Criteria) and for accrediting initial teacher-education programmes (the Graduating Teacher Standards), ...

which form the basis for provisionally registering teachers. The Registered Teacher Criteria describe the standards for quality teaching that are to be met by all fully registered teachers and guide the learning of provisionally registered teachers. The Registered Teacher Criteria focus on student learning outcomes, including teachers' analysis and use of student-assessment information, and the bicultural context in New Zealand. The NZTC, as the professional body of teachers, holds the leading role in defining standards for the profession, with the extensive involvement of the teaching profession, employers and teachers' unions.

**Sources:** Santiago et al. (2011); Nusche et al. (2012).

### *Strengthening teacher leadership*

Teachers in many countries are looking for more leadership opportunities, for leading change and not just managing what is demanded of them. In the United States, the most recent Metlife survey of teachers revealed that high numbers of teachers are eager for more leadership opportunities, even though they did not want to be principals (Markow, Macia and Lee, 2013). A study commissioned by Education International has also established a link between teacher self-efficacy and teacher leadership, and sets out proposals for a systemic approach to teacher leadership (Bangs and Frost, 2012).

By initiating improvement and innovation in schools, teacher leadership develops teachers' competence and confidence as educators, advances their professional learning, promotes change and improvement in schools, encourages professional collaboration and collegiality, and boosts professional status and recognition. In doing so, teacher leadership helps to maintain and improve teachers' commitment, self-efficacy and morale. The Ontario leadership and learning programme, the Chartered Teachers initiative in Scotland, and Teach to Lead in the United States provide just a few examples of how to organise such initiatives (Boxes 2.11, 2.12 and 2.13).

#### Box 2.11 The Ontario Teacher Leadership and Learning Programme

The Ontario Teacher Leadership and Learning Programme is an eight-year initiative, launched in 2007, to support teachers' self-directed professional development and leadership skills, and to help them share these skills with colleagues through conferences and storefronts, a virtual platform, and in collaborative activities within each school involved. The programme, developed in partnership between the Ontario Teachers' Federation and the Ontario Ministry of Education, rests on teachers designing and evaluating their own innovations and sharing what they have learned. It is particularly targeted at teachers who have been in the profession for more than four years. Each funded project lasts 18 months, and hundreds of teachers have participated in the programme.

An evaluation found that over 70% of the respondents reported that they have acquired new knowledge, improved their own practice, and developed leadership skills in facilitation and project management. Over half believed that they had increased their self-efficacy, and evaluators concluded that this percentage would be even higher if projects lasted longer and were more deliberately integrated into other schools or wider development programmes and initiatives.

**Source:** Campbell, Lieberman and Yashkina (2014).

#### Box 2.12 The Chartered Teachers initiative in Scotland

In 2006, Scotland recognised a new professional category of teachers, known as Chartered Teachers. Chartered Teacher status, earned through programmes of study and projects undertaken in teachers' own schools, aimed to recognise and reward the excellence, and encourage the continuous professional learning, of those teachers who wished to remain classroom teachers. After the completion of the qualification, teachers received a significant and lifelong salary increase. The programme was hugely popular; but in the climate of austerity pervasive in the country in subsequent years, local authorities found that the costs of the scheme were too much of a strain on their budgets. Following one of the recommendations of Teaching Scotland's Future, the Chartered Teacher scheme was discontinued in 2012.

**Source:** OECD (2015a).

**Box 2.13 Teach to Lead in the United States**

Teach to Lead (TTL) is an initiative of the US Department of Education (ED), the National Board for Professional Teaching Standards (NBPTS) and the Association for Supervision and Curriculum Development (ASCD) to advance student outcomes by expanding opportunities for teacher leadership, particularly those that allow teachers to stay in the classroom. The initiative seeks to highlight existing state and district systems that are working to support teacher leadership; share resources to create new opportunities for teacher leadership; and encourage people at all levels to commit to expanding teacher leadership.

TTL involves stakeholders at every level of education in leveraging the expertise and insight of classroom teachers. To create transformational change at the local level, TTL hosts regional Teacher Leader Summits and smaller Teacher Leader Labs in selected communities identified as having great potential for teacher leadership to take root or expand for greater impact. These meetings help to solidify stakeholders' commitment to teacher leadership and to develop detailed plans of action to achieve this goal. The initiative has engaged with more than 3 800 educators, in person and on line, and given voice to more than 875 teacher-leadership ideas in 42 states. It has helped teachers to create over 150 action plans to implement improvement projects, developed and led by teachers, to effect change at the school, district, state or national level.

Participating communities have benefitted from broad support at the local level, from open and candid dialogue about teacher leadership, and from national recognition for their work from ED, ASCD and the National Board.

**Source:** http://teachtolead.org/.

There are many other efforts to improve the quality of teachers and teaching through teacher leadership. The Norwegian GNIST initiative example (GNIST is Norwegian for "spark") is another. This national partnership between the Ministry of Education, the main stakeholders and municipalities/counties aims to increase the quality and status of the teaching profession, teacher education and school leadership. An annual teacher-recruitment campaign is a main component of the plan.

In England, the National College for Teaching and Leadership, inaugurated in 2013, is a government agency created by merging two existing bodies that worked towards school leadership and teachers' development. It aims to support development of the education workforce by creating a school-led, self-improving education system. A similar government body, the Scottish College for Educational Leadership, is being established in Scotland to provide support and coherence to leadership development across the education system at all levels of responsibility.

### *Engaging teachers in education reform*

Inviting teachers and school leaders to contribute to the development of education reforms is likely to facilitate the implementation of those reforms. Kennedy (2005) argues that highly dedicated teachers reject reform not because they are unwilling to change or improve, but because of "the sad fact that most reforms don't acknowledge the realities of classroom teaching". Some believe that imposed change creates a "culture of compliance" (Datnow and Castellano, 2000; Leithwood et al., 2002). Chapter 3 discusses, in particular, the importance of involving teachers and school leaders in the development of the appraisal processes that will be used to assess their own performance. Box 2.14 describes how a project in the Netherlands taps into teachers' own internal motivation to improve their performance.

**Box 2.14 Schools have the Initiative project in the Netherlands**

The Netherlands's Schools have the Initiative (*School aan Zet*, 2012) programme aims to leverage teachers' internal motivation to become more effective by developing skills in six areas: results-oriented work, human-resource management/learning organisation, basic skills, dealing with differences among students, gifted students, and science and technology.

Participation in this programme is voluntary and begins with schools defining their own goals and ambitions. With the help of experts to set objectives, schools can conduct three sessions, known as ambition conversations, and three evaluation conversations to monitor achievements in line with their own expectations. The programme also encourages schools to apply for funding that can be used to invite independent experts and "critical friends" to participate in these conversations. There are no specific reporting requirements connected to the funding.

**Source:** OECD (2014b).

### *Using technology*

Information and communication technology (ICT) has revolutionised virtually every aspect of life and work. Students unable to navigate through a complex digital landscape will no longer be able to participate fully in the economic, social and cultural life around them. Those responsible for educating today's "connected" learners are confronted with challenging issues, from information overload to plagiarism, from protecting children from online risks such as fraud, violations of privacy or online bullying to setting an adequate and appropriate media diet. Schools are expected to help educate children to become critical consumers of Internet services and electronic media, to make informed choices and avoid harmful behaviours. Teachers and parents are also expected to raise awareness about the risks that children face on line and how to avoid them.

And yet, analyses from PISA show that the reality lags considerably behind the promise of technology. In 2012, 96% of 15-year-old students in OECD countries reported that they have a computer at home; but only 72% reported that they use a desktop, laptop or tablet computer at school, and in some countries fewer than one in two students reported doing so. And even where computers are used in the classroom, their impact on student performance is mixed, at best. Students who use computers moderately at school tend to have somewhat better learning outcomes than students who use computers rarely. But students who use computers very frequently at school do a lot worse in most learning outcomes, even after accounting for social background and student demographics (OECD, 2015b).

The results also show no appreciable improvements in student achievement in reading, mathematics or science in the countries that had invested heavily in ICT for education. And perhaps the most disappointing finding of the report is that technology is of little help in bridging the skills divide between advantaged and disadvantaged students (OECD, 2015b). Put simply, ensuring that every child attains a baseline level of proficiency in reading and mathematics seems to do more to create equal opportunities in a digital world than can be achieved by expanding or subsidising access to high-tech devices and services.

One interpretation of all this is that building deep, conceptual understanding and higher-order thinking requires intensive teacher-student interactions, and technology sometimes distracts from this valuable human engagement. Another interpretation is that teachers have not yet become good enough at the kind of pedagogies that make the most of technology; that adding 21st-century technologies to 20th-century teaching practices just dilutes the effectiveness of teaching.

Technology allows teachers and students to access specialised materials well beyond textbooks, in multiple formats, with few constraints in time or space. It offers innovative platforms for collaboration in knowledge creation, where teachers can share and enrich teaching materials. Perhaps most important, technology can support new pedagogies that focus on learners as active participants with tools for inquiry-based pedagogies and collaborative workspaces. For example, technology can enhance experiential learning, foster project-based and inquiry-based pedagogies, facilitate hands-on activities and co-operative learning and deliver formative real-time assessments. It can also support learning and teaching communities with new tools, such as remote and virtual labs, interactive, non-linear courseware based on state-of-the-art instructional design, sophisticated software for experimentation and simulation, social media and serious games.

To deliver on the promises technology holds, countries will need a convincing strategy to build teachers' capacity to use these tools; and policy makers need to become better at building support for this agenda. Given the uncertainties that accompany all change, educators will always opt to maintain the status quo. To mobilise support for more technology-rich schools, education systems need to become better at communicating the need and building support for change. Investing in capacity development and change-management skills will be critical, and it is vital that teachers become active agents for change, not just in implementing technological innovations, but in designing them too. Box 2.15 describes a programme to fund digital technology and learning tools – and professional development for the teachers using them – in Ontario, Canada.

A school budget for training can allow schools with articulated policies for integrating ICT in teaching to put in place more economical and effective professional development at the school level. Such a budget may, for example, allow schools to organise training sessions for all teachers who use interactive whiteboards. Neighbouring schools can also organise joint training sessions for using interactive whiteboards for specific subjects if one school does not have enough teachers who teach these subjects.

Australia and England (United Kingdom) have introduced "middle-management" positions within schools that give some teachers a lead role in some subject or programme area of the school. One of these areas could be using ICT in the classroom.

Fellowship programmes can also provide recognition for lead teachers without creating permanent and formal leadership positions. Experience as a "lead user" or "ICT champion" can be considered an important asset when identifying school leaders; that will give teachers an extra incentive to take on this role.

While peer learning is an effective mode of professional development, formal in-service training is also valuable, particularly when teachers have opportunities to practice what they have learned in the training. However, this form of training tends to be more costly, both for the public purse and in terms of time and energy for schools and teachers.

### Box 2.15 **21st-Century Teaching and Learning Strategy in Ontario, Canada**

Through its Technology and Learning Fund (TLF), Ontario is investing CAD 150 million over three years in digital technology and learning tools as well as professional learning for educators. School boards must use their TLF funding to support deeper learning by: creating more teacher-student learning partnerships through real-world, authentic learning tasks enabled by technology; providing more opportunities for peer-to-peer learning through technology; developing and providing professional learning about new assessment practices that reflect deep learning pedagogy; and providing opportunities to develop new learning partnerships among educators through technology in addition to face-to-face professional development.

The TLF includes funding for boards to engage in 21st-century innovation research projects that are developing deeper learning teaching practices. School boards have been scaling up these practices over the past four years. The fund also provides additional funding to support a Technology Enabled Learning and Teaching (TELT) contact in every school board. Their core work is to advance the transformation of learning and teaching in a physical and virtual environment.

Ontario is also committed to defining 21st-century competencies, such as critical thinking, communication, collaboration, creativity and entrepreneurship, to inform curriculum renewal. To this end, the Ontario Ministry of Education has developed a draft 21st-century Competencies Foundation Document summarising the international and Ontario research on deeper learning and 21st-century competencies. In addition, Ontario is working with provinces across Canada to identify pan-Canadian 21st-century competencies.

**Source:** Ministry of Education, Ontario, Canada.

## References


**Bangs J.** and **D. Frost** (2012), *Teacher Self-efficacy, Voice and Leadership: Towards a Policy Framework for Education International, a Report on an International Survey of the Views of Teachers and Teacher Union Officials,* Education International Research Institute. Cambridge University, Leadership for Learning, http://download.ei-ie.org/Docs/WebDepot/teacher_self-efficacy_voice_leadership.pdf.

**Blondin, C.** and **B. Giot** (2011), *Cadres d'évaluation en vue d'améliorer les résultats scolaires – Étude thématique de l'OCDE : Rapport de base pour la Communauté française de Belgique*, Ministère de la Fédération Wallonie-Bruxelles, www.oecd.org/fr/edu/scolaire/49048280.pdf.

**Campbell, C., A. Lieberman** and **A. Yashkina,** (2014), "The Teacher Learning and Leadership Program: Research report 2013-14", Ontario Teachers' Federation, Toronto, ON.

**Chong, W.H.** and **C.A. Kong** (2012), "Teacher collaborative learning and teacher self-efficacy: The case of lesson study", *Journal of Experimental Education*, Vol. 80/3, pp. 263-283.

**Cordingley, P.** et al. (2015), *Developing Great Teaching: Lessons from the International Reviews into Effective Professional Development*, Teacher Development Trust, London, www.tdtrust.org/wp-content/uploads/2015/10/DGT-Full-report.pdf.

**Darling-Hammond, L.** and **A. Lieberman** (eds.) (2013), *High Quality Teaching and Learning: Changing Policies and Practices*, Routledge, London.

**Datnow, A.** and **M. Castellano** (2000), "Teachers' responses to success for all: How beliefs, experiences and adaptation shape implementation", *American Educational Research Journal*, Vol. 37/3, pp. 775-799.

**Education Commission of the States** (2004), *Professional Development, Pros and Cons: What Does the Evidence Say?*, Education Commission of the States, Denver, CO.

**Evans, L.** (2008), "Professionalism, professionality and the development of education professionals", *British Journal of Educational Studies*, Vol. 56/1, pp. 20-38.

**Flemish Ministry of Education and Training** and **the University of Antwerp Edubron Research Group** (2010), *OECD Review on Evaluation and Assessment Frameworks for Improving School Outcomes: Country Background Report for the Flemish Community of Belgium*, OECD, Paris, www.oecd.org/edu/school/46974684.pdf.

**Fournier, G.** and **D. Mildon** (forthcoming), *OECD Review on Evaluation and Assessment Frameworks for Improving School Outcomes: Country Background Report for Canada*, Council of Ministers of Education, Canada (CMEC).

**Frost, D.** et al. (2016), "A profession-led master's programme: A breakthrough in support for school and teacher development", a paper presented in the symposium: *The empowerment of teachers as agents of change*, ICSEI, Glasgow, 6-9 January 2016.

**Gilmore, A.** (2008), *Assessment Review Paper 8: Professional Learning in Assessment*, Ministry of Education, Wellington.

**Glazerman, S.** et al. (2010), *Impacts of Comprehensive Teacher Induction: Final Results from a Randomized Controlled Study*, NCEE 2010-4027, National Center for Education Evaluation and Regional Assistance, Institute of Education Sciences, US Department of Education, Washington, DC.

**Hargreaves, D.** (2004), "Policy for educational innovation in the knowledge-driven economy" in OECD, *Innovation in the Knowledge-Based Economy: Implications for Education and Learning Systems*, Knowledge management, OECD Publishing, Paris, http://dx.doi.org/10.1787/9789264105621-en.

**Hopfenbeck, T.** et al. (2013), "Balancing trust and accountability? The assessment for learning programme in Norway: A Governing Complex Education Systems case study", *OECD Education Working Papers*, No. 97, OECD Publishing, Paris, http://dx.doi.org/10.1787/5k3txnpqlsnn-en.

**Ingersoll, R.M.** and **M. Strong** (2011), "The impact of induction and mentoring programs for beginning teachers: A critical review of research", *Review of Educational Research*, Vol. 81/2, pp. 201-233.

**Jensen B., J. Sonnemann, K. Roberts-Hull** and **A. Hunter** (2016), *Beyond PD: Teacher Professional Learning in High-Performing Systems*, National Center on Education and the Economy, Washington, DC, www.ncee.org/beyondpd/.

**Kennedy, M.** (2005), *Inside Teaching*, Harvard University Press, London.

**Kim, K.** et al. (2010), *OECD Review on Evaluation and Assessment Frameworks for Improving School Outcomes: Country Background Report for Korea*, Korean Educational Development Institute (KEDI), Seoul, www.oecd.org/education/school/49363138.pdf.

**Lai, M.** and **Lo, N.** (2007), "Teacher professionalism in educational reform: The experience of Hong-Kong and Shanghai", *Compare*, Vol. 37/1, pp. 53-68.

**Leithwood, K., R. Steinbach** and **D. Jantzi** (2002), "School leadership and teachers' motivation to implement accountability policies", *Educational Administration Quarterly*, Vol. 38/1, pp. 94-119.

**Liaw, E.C.** (2009), "Teacher efficacy of pre-service teachers in Taiwan: The influence of classroom teaching and group discussions", *Teaching and Teacher Education*, Vol. 25, pp. 176-180.

**LoCasale-Crouch, J.** et al. (2012), "The role of the mentor in supporting new teachers: Associations with self-efficacy, reflection, and quality", *Mentoring and Tutoring: Partnership in Learning*, Vol. 20/3, pp. 303-323.

**Markow, D., L. Macia** and **H. Lee,** (2013), *The Metlife Survey of the American Teacher, Challenges for School Leadership, A Survey of Teachers and Principals*, conducted for Metlife Inc.

**Mazurkiewicz, G., B. Walczak** and **M. Jewdokimow** (2014), "Implementation of a new school supervision system in Poland: A Governing Complex Education Systems Case Study", *OECD Education Working Papers*, No. 111, OECD Publishing, Paris, http://dx.doi.org/10.1787/5jxrlxrxgc6b-en.

**Michaelowa, K.** (2002), *Teacher Job Satisfaction, Student Achievement, and the Cost of Primary Education in Francophone Sub-Saharan Africa*, Hamburg Institute of International Economics.

**National Commission on Teaching and America's Future** (1996), *What Matters Most: Teaching for America's Future*, National Commission on Teaching and America's Future, New York, NY.

**National Institute of Education, Singapore** (2009), *TE21: A Teacher Education Model for the 21st Century*, National Institute of Education, Singapore.

**Nitsche, S.** et al. (2013), "Teachers' professional goal orientations: Importance for further training and sick leave", *Learning and Individual Differences*, Vol. 23, pp. 272-278.

**Nusche, D.** et al. (2012), *OECD Reviews of Evaluation and Assessment in Education: New Zealand 2011*, OECD Reviews of Evaluation and Assessment in Education, OECD Publishing, Paris, http://dx.doi.org/10.1787/9789264116917-en.

**Nusche, D.** et al. (2011), *OECD Reviews of Evaluation and Assessment in Education: Norway 2011*, OECD Reviews of Evaluation and Assessment in Education, OECD Publishing, Paris, http://dx.doi.org/10.1787/9789264117006-en.

**OECD** (2015a), *Improving Schools in Scotland: An OECD Perspective*, OECD Education Policy Reviews, OECD, Paris, www.oecd.org/education/school/Improving-Schools-in-Scotland-An-OECD-Perspective.pdf.

**OECD** (2015b), *Students, Computers and Learning: Making the Connection,* PISA, OECD Publishing, Paris, http://dx.doi.org/10.1787/9789264239555-en.

**OECD** (2014a), *Lessons from PISA for Korea*, Strong Performers and Successful Reformers in Education, OECD Publishing, Paris, http://dx.doi.org/10.1787/9789264190672-en.

**OECD** (2014b), *Education Policy Outlook: The Netherlands*, OECD, Paris, www.oecd.org/edu/EDUCATION%20POLICY%20OUTLOOK_NETHERLANDS_EN%20.pdf.

**OECD** (2013a), *PISA 2012 Results: What Makes Schools Successful (Volume IV): Resources, Policies and Practices*, PISA, OECD Publishing, Paris, http://dx.doi.org/10.1787/9789264201156-en.

**OECD** (2013b), *Synergies for Better Learning: An International Perspective on Evaluation and Assessment,* OECD Reviews of Evaluation and Assessment in Education, OECD Publishing, Paris, http://dx.doi.org/10.1787/9789264190658-en.

**Ofsted** (Office for Standards in Education) (2006), "The logical chain: Continuing professional development in effective schools", OFSTED Publications No. 2639, United Kingdom.

**Pont B., D. Nusche** and **H. Moorman** (2008), *Improving School Leadership – Volume 1: Policy and Practice*, OECD Publishing, Paris, http://dx.doi.org/10.1787/9789264044715-en.

**Puchner, L.D.** and **A.R. Taylor** (2006), "Lesson study, collaboration and teacher efficacy: Stories from two-school based math lesson study groups", *Teaching and Teacher Education*, Vol. 22, pp. 922-934.

**Rockoff, J.** (2008), "Does mentoring reduce turnover and improve skills of new employees? Evidence from teachers in New York City", www0.gsb.columbia.edu/faculty/jrockoff/rockoff_mentoring_february_08.pdf.

**Ross, J.** and **C. Bruce** (2007), "Teacher self-assessment: A mechanism for facilitating professional growth", *Teaching and Teacher Education*, Vol. 23, pp. 146-159.

**Sahlberg, P.** (2010), "The secret to Finland's success: Educating teachers", Stanford Center for Opportunity Policy in Education – Research Brief, September 2010, Stanford, CA, https://edpolicy.stanford.edu/sites/default/files/publications/secret-finland%E2%80%99s-success-educating-teachers.pdf.

**Santiago, P.** et al. (2013), *Teacher Evaluation in Chile 2013*, OECD Reviews of Evaluation and Assessment in Education, OECD Publishing, Paris, http://dx.doi.org/10.1787/9789264172616-en.

**Santiago, P.** et al. (2012), *OECD Reviews of Evaluation and Assessment in Education: Mexico 2012,* OECD Reviews of Evaluation and Assessment in Education, OECD Publishing, Paris, http://dx.doi.org/10.1787/9789264172647-en.

**Santiago, P.** et al. (2011), *OECD Reviews of Evaluation and Assessment in Education: Australia*, OECD Reviews of Evaluation and Assessment in Education, OECD Publishing, Paris, http://dx.doi.org/10.1787/9789264116672-en.

**Shewbridge, C.** et al. (2011), *OECD Reviews of Evaluation and Assessment in Education: Denmark*, OECD Reviews of Evaluation and Assessment in Education, OECD Publishing, Paris, http://dx.doi.org/10.1787/9789264116597-en.

**Siegrist, H.** (2015), "Profession and Professionalization, History of", in J.D. Wright (ed.), *International Encyclopedia of Social and Behavioral Sciences*, 2nd Edition, Elsevier, Philadelphia, PA, pp. 95-100, http://dx.doi.org/10.1016/B978-0-08-097086-8.62020-2.

**Thoonen, E.E.J.** et al. (2011), "How to improve teaching practices: The role of teacher motivation, organizational factors, and leadership practices", *Educational Administration Quarterly*, Vol. 47/3, pp. 496-536.

**Timperley, H.** (2011), "A background paper to inform the development of a national professional development framework for teachers and school leaders", Australian Institute for Teaching and School Leadership, Melbourne.

**Timperley, H.** et al. (2008), *Teacher Professional Learning and Development: Best Evidence Synthesis Iteration (BES)*, New Zealand Ministry of Education, Wellington.

**Tschannen-Moran, M.** and **P. McMaster** (2009), "Sources of self-efficacy: Four professional development formats and their relationship to self-efficacy and implementation of a new teaching strategy", *The Elementary School Journal*, Vol. 110/2, pp. 228-245.

**Villegas-Reimers, E.** (2003), *Teacher Professional Development: An International Review of the Literature*, UNESCO, International Institute for Educational Planning, Paris.

**Webb** et al. (2004), "A comparative analysis of primary teacher professionalism in England and Finland", *Comparative education*, Vol. 40/1, pp. 83-107.

**Wininger, S.R.** and **P.M. Birkholz** (2013), "Sources of instructional feedback, job satisfaction, and basic psychological needs", *Innovative Higher Education*, Vol. 38, pp. 159-170.

Chapter 3

# WHAT CAN GOVERNMENTS DO TO IMPLEMENT EDUCATION POLICIES EFFECTIVELY?

Education reform will not happen unless educators endorse and implement it. This chapter discusses some of the actions that could help turn policies into practice, including acknowledging divergent views and interests, communicating the rationale for reform, fostering consensus, engaging stakeholders – including teachers – in designing and implementing policies, ensuring there is sufficient capacity and resources, and building partnerships with education unions to design and implement the reforms. The chapter presents examples of related initiatives from around the world.

Implementing reform of any kind, in any sector, is never easy; but it is particularly difficult in the education sector. One reason is simply the scale of the sector:

- Public spending on institutions alone (excluding financial support for students and families) is one of the biggest areas of public spending outside transfers (OECD, 2015).
- Virtually everyone has participated in education and has an opinion about it.
- Education is widely present and visible: almost every community has a school it can call its own, and higher education and training institutions are increasingly part of the local landscape and a presence in the workplace.

As a result, there are a lot of stakeholders in education who have a vested interest in maintaining the status quo. Even small reforms can involve massive reallocations of resources, and touch the lives of millions on both the client and provider sides. This rules out "reform by stealth" and makes it essential to have consensus, or at least broad political support, for any proposed reform. In essence, education reform will not happen unless educators endorse and implement it.

Implementation of education reform is influenced by many of the same factors that influence implementation in other sectors. There is uncertainty about the size and distribution of benefits. But uncertainty is a particularly vexed issue in education reform because of the range of actors (including students, parents, teachers, employers and trade unions) who have stakes in education outcomes. Uncertainty about costs is problematic because education infrastructure is large and implicates multiple levels of government, each often trying to minimise or shift the costs of reform.

To some extent, these challenges are typical of the obstacles facing reformers in many domains. However, assessing the relative costs and benefits in education is rendered particularly difficult by the large number of intervening variables that influence the nature, size and distribution of benefits of reform. In short, it is rarely possible to predict clear, identifiable links between policies and outcomes, especially given the time lags involved.

The issue of loss of advantages or privileged positions is of particular importance in education reform, because the vast structure of established (usually public) providers implies the existence of extensive vested interests. The resistance of provider interests to reform may well be more acute in education than in other sectors (except, perhaps, for healthcare) for a number of reasons. Teachers are generally viewed positively by the public, even when there is great dissatisfaction with education systems. They often command greater public trust than politicians, so any resistance to reform on their part is likely to be effective. The implementation of reforms is often impossible without the co-operation of the providers. They can easily undermine reforms in the implementation phase, while blaming policy makers for having attempted misguided reforms in the first place. Last but not least, teachers in many OECD countries are well organised.

Timing is relevant to education reform in two senses. First and most obviously, there is a substantial gap between the time at which the initial cost of reform is incurred, and the time when it is evident whether the intended benefits of reforms actually materialise. While timing complicates the politics of reform in many domains, it seems to have a greater impact on education reform, where the lags involved are far longer than is typical of, for example, labour- or product-market reforms. As a result, the political cycle may have a direct impact on the timing, scope and content of education reform. Education reform becomes a thankless task when elections take place before the benefits are realised.

Timing can be important also with regard to the sequencing of different components of reform. For example, one element – curriculum reform, for example – might require prior reform in pre-service and in-service training in order to be effective.

However, there are strong countervailing forces pushing for a shake-up of the status quo. At a micro level, education plays an important part in determining employability and earnings; at a macro level, it is associated with higher levels of productivity and growth. The emergence of the knowledge society and the upward trend in skill requirements in the labour market only increases the importance of education. And the cost of underperformance and underinvestment in education also is rising.

As a result, the circle of those who feel they are directly affected by the outcomes of education has broadened beyond parents and students to employers and virtually anyone who has a stake in social and economic welfare. These forces also make stakeholders more demanding. Strategies to overcome resistance to education reforms are similar in certain respects to those adopted in other areas. Reform is more easily undertaken in "crisis" conditions, although the meaning of "crisis" may be somewhat different in education. The shock involved is likely to be something that radically and abruptly alters perceptions of the education system rather than an event that suddenly affects its ability to function.

The release in December 2001 of the first OECD Programme for International Student Assessment (PISA) results (OECD, 2001) sent shockwaves through Denmark because they undermined the widely shared but unsubstantiated view that Denmark had one of the best education systems in the world. PISA provided robust evidence that the system was, in fact, close to the OECD average and fairly inequitable. After considerable soul-searching and an expert review by the OECD, the Danish government launched a far-reaching reform of primary and lower secondary education (Danish Ministry of Education and Rambøll, 2011).

"Crisis" often takes other forms in education. It can be the slow-building, but relentless, pressures imposed by demographic changes. For example, the prospect of fewer upper secondary school graduates forced the government of Finland, only a few years after it created a new polytechnic sector, to launch ambitious reforms to reduce the number of tertiary institutions and alter how they were governed and financed. In Germany, smaller populations of school-aged children forced some *Länder* to merge education tracks at the secondary level (*Realschule* and *Hauptschule*).

## THE DIFFICULTY OF CO-ORDINATING REFORM IN COMPLEX EDUCATION SYSTEMS

As in other sectors, co-ordinated reforms in discrete parts of education systems have proven to be mutually reinforcing. This was the case in Scotland when the government, intending to initiate sweeping reforms to curricula, testing and leadership, started with an overhaul of teacher training, induction and pay. The success of reforms in curricula and testing were seen as hinging on prior reforms that would have an influence on who teaches and how they are trained (OECD, 2008).

However, given that education systems involve multiple levels of government, implementation of "comprehensive reform" may be difficult to co-ordinate across the various levels of the administration, and across multiple regional and local jurisdictions. This problem was encountered in Denmark, where it has been difficult to synchronise reforms to strengthen national testing with the pre- and in-service training of teachers employed by municipalities (Nusche, Wurzburg and Naughton, 2010).

The United States shares with many other federal systems (Australia, Austria, Germany, Switzerland and the United Kingdom) a different kind of challenge in attempting to address the problem of weak student performance. Though the federal government can require states to set quality standards as a condition for receiving federal money for education, it cannot determine what those standards are. It was only in 2009 that state school officials and governors agreed on the principle of establishing national, common, core standards in English language and mathematics.

More generally, there are several features of education systems that need to be considered when contemplating reform:

**Specific capacity constraints.** Overcoming resistance to reform will be a wasted effort if systems do not have state-of-the-art knowledge, professional know-how and adequate institutional arrangements to support dissemination of information and lessons about the new tasks and responsibilities inherent in the reforms. Successful reform may require significant investment in staff development, or clustering reforms to build capacity in related institutions.

**General capacity considerations.** In knowledge-based societies, the increased importance of human capital is reflected in a greater demand for education at all levels, although in some countries declining birth rates have reduced participation rates. Internal and international migration can add to the challenge of anticipating and responding to changes in demand for education.

**Complex governance**. Education systems extend from local schools and independent universities to national ministries. The responsibilities of institutions and different levels of government vary from country to country, as do the relative importance and independence of non-public providers. Reforms need to take into account the respective responsibilities of different actors. Some reforms, particularly those related to strengthening accountability for the performance of the education system, may only be possible if responsibilities can be reallocated.

**Greater availability of performance data**. As obtaining, managing and accessing information has become cheaper, there has been an explosion of information on the performance of education systems, down to the level of the individual classroom and student. A political trend towards increasing accountability for public services has spurred greater interest in benchmarking performance, locally, nationally and internationally, allowing for more "evidence-based" policy making.

Education ministries have been on the front line of some of the most visible public policy reforms on issues related to improving quality, the status of teachers, strengthening accountability, managing capacity in the face of declining school-age populations and participation rates, and controlling and financing the cost of mass participation in higher education.

Education policy makers know only too well the difficulty of securing stable financing for expanding tertiary education, whether by reallocating funding from other areas of public expenditure, or imposing tuition fees. Reforms that entail more testing of students often encounter resistance from teachers concerned about external accountability. Reforms to advance or delay vocational studies may be resisted by parents who are sceptical about whether promised benefits will materialise.

## SOME LESSONS ON IMPLEMENTING EDUCATION REFORM

Several policy lessons have emerged from OECD countries that have implemented reforms in education:

- Policy makers need to build consensus about the aims of education reform and engage stakeholders, especially teachers, in formulating and implementing policy responses.
- External pressures can be used to build a compelling case for change.
- All political players and stakeholders need to develop realistic expectations about the pace and nature of reforms to improve outcomes.
- Reforms need to be backed by sustainable financing.
- There is some shift away from reform initiatives per se towards building self-adjusting systems with feedback at all levels, incentives to react and tools to strengthen capacities to deliver better outcomes. Investment is needed in change-management skills. Teachers need reassurance that they will be given the tools to change and the recognition of their professional motivation to improve their students' outcomes.
- Evidence from international assessments, national surveys and inspectorates can be used to guide policy making. Evidence is most helpful when it is fed back to institutions along with information and tools about how they can use the information to improve outcomes.
- "Whole-of-government" approaches can include education in more comprehensive reforms. These need to be co-ordinated with all the relevant ministries.

### *Acknowledge divergent views and interests*

A diversity of views makes the policy-making exercise particularly challenging, especially given that policy makers often represent one of the stakeholder groups – the government authorities. For example, in the choice of teacher appraisal methods, there is a particularly contentious debate about the relative importance of the summative and formative purposes of such appraisals. On the one hand, policy makers and parents tend to value quality assurance and accountability. "They make the point that public schools are, after all, public institutions, supported by taxpayer money, and that the public has a legitimate interest in the quality of the teaching that occurs there. It is through the system of teacher evaluation that members of the public, their legislators, local boards of education and administrators ensure the quality of teaching" (Danielson and McGreal, 2000). On the other hand, teachers and their unions tend to prefer formative systems of appraisal with limited potential for external accountability (Avalos and Assael, 2006).

However, those divergent views can be accommodated. The Czech Republic, for example, began developing a standardised section of the school-leaving examination in 1997, but the section was only introduced 14 years later, in 2011. During this time, several models were developed, pilot versions were implemented, fundamental features were modified several times and the reforms were hotly debated, particularly among the country's political parties, which could not reach consensus on the approach to the examination (Santiago et al., 2012).

### *Communicate the rationale for reform*

Another priority is to clearly communicate a long-term vision of what is to be accomplished for student learning. Individuals and groups are more likely to accept changes that are not necessarily in their own best interests if they and society at large understand the reasons for these changes and can see the role they should play within the broad national strategy. The evidence base of the underlying policy diagnosis, research findings on alternative policy options and their likely impact, and information on the costs of reform versus inaction should all be disseminated widely, not just to the stakeholders with a direct interest.

For instance, in order to bring teachers on board for reforms of standardised student tests, it is critical that teachers understand and support the assessment goals (Hamilton and Stecher, 2002; Alliance for Excellent Education, 2010). Establishing clear goals and standards and communicating them to teachers mitigates behaviours such as "teaching to the test", as teachers have a clearer sense of the kinds of student outcomes they should be trying to achieve (Hamilton and Stecher, 2002).

Resistance to reform might also be due to imperfect information, either on the nature of the proposed policy changes, their impact, or whether or not the stakeholders involved – including the general public – will be better or worse off

at the individual or group level. The public may be unprepared for some reforms, resulting in a lack of social acceptance for policy innovations. This might be exacerbated by an underdeveloped culture of evaluation in education. Thus it is important to make the evidence underlying the policy proposals available to the relevant stakeholders to help convince educators and society at large. The objective is to raise awareness of problematic issues, enhance the national debate and disseminate evidence on the effectiveness and impact of different policy alternatives, and hence to find a consensus on evaluation policy.

In the case of teacher appraisal, Milanowski and Heneman (2001) found that teachers' receptiveness towards a newly implemented system of teacher appraisal in a medium-sized school district in the United States was correlated with acceptance of the teaching standards, the perceived fairness of the process, the qualities of the evaluator, and the perception that the evaluation system has a positive impact on their teaching.

In 2007, Portugal's Ministry of Education set up the Scientific Council for Teacher Evaluation (CCAP) as a consultative body to supervise and monitor the implementation of a teacher-appraisal system. The CCAP was composed of education researchers and distinguished teachers and, as such, was in a good position to recognise good evaluation practices, be informed of relevant research developments and provide evidence-based advice (Santiago et al., 2009).

In Hungary, the Council for the Evaluation of Public Education, established in 2004, is an advisory body of the Ministry of Education and Culture that seeks to bring scientific evidence to the decision-making processes within the education system. Its members, invited by the Minister of Education and Culture, are among the most prestigious national and international academic experts in areas such as the appraisal of teacher effectiveness, measurement theory, data collection and data analysis, content framework development and the management of evaluation programmes (Hungarian Ministry of Education and Culture, 2010).

Box 3.1 describes how a communications policy changed the nature of the conversation about education reform in the US state of Rhode Island.

### Box 3.1 Communication strategies between US states and districts

With about half of the funding for the national Race to the Top programme – nearly USD 2 billion – going directly to districts, state education agencies (SEAs) focused on building capacity to systematically support districts and schools in their improvement efforts. SEAs supported districts' efforts to collect and analyse data to assess progress in meeting state and local goals, and established new routines to communicate and receive better information from their districts about how things were working on the ground.

For example, the SEA in Rhode Island formed cohorts of district leaders to meet every three months with state leaders and with each other – a process that promoted peer learning to resolve key implementation issues. District progress reports became a component of state programme meetings during which senior leaders discussed the progress of projects explicitly in terms of the district's experience. The SEA made adjustments based on this feedback. For example, the Rhode Island Department of Education altered its communication strategies for a number of state initiatives based on feedback that the previous communication was confusing. Through this process, state and district leaders reported they experienced "a culture shift," as they "moved from a compliance-oriented approach to an approach that emphasizes systematic reflection, collaboration, problem-solving and ongoing communication between [the Rhode Island Department of Education] and our districts." State leaders in every Race to the Top state interacted with district leaders, principals and teachers regularly to better understand the realities of implementation and create support to meet local needs.

**Source:** US Department of Education.

### *Foster consensus*

There is extensive evidence that consensus is conducive to successful implementation of policy reforms. At the same time, given the diversity of stakeholders in education, consensus can lead to agreement at the level of the lowest common denominator, which may be insufficient to lead to genuine improvement. As noted by Fiske (1996) with respect to school decentralisation, researchers are almost unanimous in arguing that if school decentralisation is going to be successful and have a positive impact on the quality of teaching and learning, it must be built on a foundation of broad consensus among the various actors involved and the various interest groups affected by such a change. In fact, he observes that countries where leaders sought to build consensus for reform are those where decentralisation was most successful.

Consensus can be fostered through proposals and feedback that allow legitimate concerns to be taken into account, and thus reduce the likelihood of strong opposition by some stakeholder groups. Regular involvement by stakeholders in policy design helps to build capacity and shared ideas over time. There is broad agreement in the literature that the involvement of stakeholders in education policy development cultivates a sense of joint ownership over policies, and hence helps build consensus over both the need and the relevance of reforms (Finlay et al., 1998; OECD, 2007). Policies promoting consensus build trust between the various stakeholder groups and policy makers. Keating (2011) analysed how various school districts in the United States developed and implemented new school-principal appraisal systems. In most school districts, collaboration between different stakeholders (e.g. unions, teachers, school leaders and community representatives) played a key role in the design and implementation stages. The setting of shared priorities, negotiation, consensus building and transparency often resulted in greater ownership and acceptance among stakeholders.

The experience of OECD countries suggests that mechanisms of regular and institutionalised consultation – which are inherent to consensual policy making – contribute to the development of trust among parties, and help them reach consensus. In Denmark, following the 2004 OECD recommendations on the need to establish an evaluation culture, all major stakeholder groups agreed on the importance of working to this end (their efforts were documented in "The *Folkeskole*'s response to the OECD" [Danish Ministry of Education and Rambøll, 2011]). Box 3.2 outlines a range of initiatives in Denmark for promoting dialogue and reaching common views on evaluation policies in education.

### Box 3.2 Promoting dialogue and reaching common views on evaluation in education (Denmark)

In Denmark, there is a general tradition of involving the relevant interest groups in developing policies for primary and lower secondary schools (*Folkeskole*). The key interest groups include education authorities at the central level, municipalities (local government), teachers (Danish Union of Teachers), school leaders/principals (Danish School Principals' Union), parents (National Parents' Association), students, the association for municipal management in the area of schools, associations representing the interests of the independent (private) primary schools in Denmark, and researchers. The Council for Evaluation and Quality Development of Primary and Lower Secondary Education is the most prominent platform for dialogue in relation to evaluation and assessment policies among these interest groups. It works on collecting and disseminating the most important research results. A range of other initiatives helped to promote dialogue and consensus on education evaluation:

A reference group was set up to guide the project "Strengthening of the evaluation culture in the *Folkeskole*". The reference group, whose membership includes all the relevant stakeholder groups, meets on a regular basis to discuss the project. This includes, for instance, the development of national student tests.

The interest groups of the *Folkeskole* were involved in 2010-11 in a committee established by the Minister of Education aiming at deregulating the *Folkeskole*.

In 2007-08, the Danish Union of Teachers and the Ministry of Education collaborated on a project called "The School of the Month". Each month, a school was celebrated for remarkable results. The project has since been pursued under the heading "the good example of the month" (www.skolestyrelsen.dk).

The Local Government Denmark project "Partnership on the *Folkeskole*", involving 34 municipalities, has been a platform for co-operation and reflection among municipalities (www.kl.dk/ImageVault/Images/id_40353/ImageVaultHandler.aspx).

The Quality and Supervision Agency in collaboration with the Danish Evaluation Institute carry out "inspirational seminars" for teachers and school pedagogical staff with the aim of encouraging schools to develop evaluation activities.

The Quality and Supervision Agency has all major stakeholder groups represented in focus groups, which are summoned on a regular basis to provide input on different initiatives related to strengthening the evaluation culture in the *Folkeskole*.

The different interest groups of the *Folkeskole* regularly launch common actions and/or common proposals related to issues in the *Folkeskole*, e.g. a paper with the title Common knowledge – Common action.

**Source:** Danish Ministry of Education and Rambøll (2011).

At the heart of the New Zealand education system is strong trust in the professionalism of all actors and a culture of consultation and dialogue. Overall, the development of the national evaluation and assessment agenda has been characterised by strong collaborative work, as opposed to prescriptions being imposed from above. As a result of this participative approach, there appears to be considerable agreement and commitment of schools to overall evaluation and assessment strategies. While there are differences of views, there seems to be an underlying consensus on the purposes of evaluation and an expectation among stakeholders to participate in shaping the national agenda (Nusche et al., 2012).

Similarly, policy making in Norway is characterised by a high level of respect for local ownership. This is evident in the development of the national evaluation and assessment framework. School owners and schools have a high degree of autonomy regarding school policies, curriculum development and evaluation and assessment. There is a shared understanding that democratic decision making and buy-in from those concerned by evaluation and assessment policy are essential for successful implementation (Nusche et al., 2011).

In Finland, the objectives and priorities for education evaluation are determined in the Education Evaluation Plan, which is devised by the Ministry of Education and Culture in collaboration with the Education Evaluation Council, the Higher Education Evaluation Council, the National Board of Education and other key groups. The members of the Education Evaluation Council represent the education administration, education providers, teachers, students, employers, employees and researchers, and thus can influence the aims and priorities of evaluation systems (Finnish Ministry of Education and Culture, forthcoming).

A "Monitoring Commission" (*Commission de Pilotage*) in the French Community of Belgium was given a key role in monitoring the education system. It has two main missions: co-ordinate and review the coherence of the education system, and follow the implementation of pedagogical reforms. Its membership reflects all the relevant actors in the education system: school inspectors, school organisers, researchers, teachers' unions and parents' representatives (Blondin and Giot, 2011).

When new policies are introduced, a combination of top-down and bottom-up initiatives generally fosters consensus (Finlay et al., 1998). For instance, a study of evidence-informed policy making underlines how the involvement of practitioners – teachers, other education staff and their unions – in producing, interpreting and translating research evidence into policy gives these practitioners a strong sense of ownership and strengthens their confidence in the reform process (OECD, 2007). In the Flemish Community of Belgium, the Flemish Education Council (VLOR) is an independent advisory body that the Ministry of Education and Training is required to consult when a draft decree is prepared for the Parliament. The council brings together representatives of school organisers, school leaders, teachers, researchers, students and parents (Flemish Ministry of Education and Training and the University of Antwerp, Edubron Research Group, 2010).

System-wide consultations can be major facilitators of reform. Box 3.3 provides two recent examples from Chile and Italy in which extensive consultations laid the foundations for fundamental changes in teacher policy. Box 3.4 describes how the national Race to the Top programme in the United States encourages individual states to create their own vision for improving teaching and learning, and to support all the individuals in their education system to act on that vision in ways that made sense at the local level.

### Box 3.3 Consultation and teacher policy reform in Chile and Italy

**Chile**

The Teachers' Act of 1991 was designed to introduce teacher evaluation systems in elementary and secondary schools. The scheme allowed employers to dismiss teachers who were negatively evaluated two years in a row. This evaluation system, however, had not been implemented because of objections from the Teachers' Association about the composition of the evaluation committees, and the fact that the system focused on punishment rather than improvement. However, teacher evaluation continued to be a topic of public and political concern throughout the 1990s. In response, the Minister of Education established a technical committee comprising representatives of the ministry, the municipalities and the Teachers' Association. After several months, the committee reached agreement on a model for teacher evaluation. At the same time, its members agreed to prepare guidelines for standards of professional performance and to implement a pilot project in several areas of the country to evaluate and adjust the procedures and instruments to be used. After wide consultations throughout the country and agreement with the teaching profession, a framework for performance standards was developed and officially approved. The pilot project for teacher performance evaluation has been applied in four regions. In June 2003, the ministry, the municipalities and the Teachers' Association signed an agreement that established the progressive application of the new evaluation system.

...

**Italy**

In March 2003, major new legislation, *General regulations on education and basic level of performance regarding education and professional training,* was passed by the Italian Parliament. The legislation is considered a landmark in the decentralisation of education, and involves a new focus on outcomes and quality. In order to pass this new legislation, numerous political activities and debates were undertaken throughout Italy, including with stakeholders, community groups and experts. Committee members also contacted citizens directly, through e-mail. Parents were a particular focus of the legislation, with initiatives to improve school choice, provide better-quality information, and strengthen school and system accountability. The legislation also encompassed the establishment of a national evaluation system, and changes to initial and in-service teacher education requirements. The process took place over 18 months and the wide consultations were seen as vital in building the momentum for change.

**Source:** OECD (2005).

### Box 3.4 The changing role of states in US education

State education agencies (SEAs) that applied for a Race to the Top grant had to articulate a comprehensive and coherent plan to improve student achievement and secure buy-in and commitments from many stakeholders, including the governor, the state board of education, and local school districts that would work with them to implement the plan.

Many SEAs had never attempted to work this closely with their districts to implement specific initiatives to improve teaching and learning before Race to the Top. In many states, a teacher or district leader's experience with its SEA had been a one-way street. Top-down policy memos or directives on training requirements may have been the only ways the agency in charge of overseeing education in their state had communicated with teachers. District leaders may have had little interaction with their SEA beyond notifications that funds were available for their schools or that reviews and audits would be conducted to ensure that rules were being followed.

While SEA staff had the skills and knowledge to ensure compliance with federal and state laws and regulations (e.g. tracking compliance with timelines and holding districts accountable for adhering to established processes), different skills were needed to implement their Race to the Top plans. Forging new, closer partnerships with their local education agencies, SEAs built the knowledge and skills of their staff and recruited new staff to drive comprehensive and collaborative change in their education system. For example, SEA staff had to work in partnership with district staff to support their lowest-performing schools and improve data systems to meet the needs of teachers and leaders. Rather than receiving updates from district staff on a monthly or quarterly basis, SEA staff often needed to work side-by-side with district staff on an ongoing basis to identify and solve practical implementation issues.

When local education agencies and schools encountered challenges, Race to the Top SEAs responded by seeking creative solutions to meet local needs. For example, Georgia made hundreds of tweaks to its statewide data system based on teacher feedback during the first years of use. The state continues to receive and act upon teacher feedback regularly as it develops new data reports and makes its data system easier to use.

Delaware and Tennessee had initially planned to conduct large-scale training sessions to help teachers transition to new standards. However, after soliciting feedback from teachers, they changed their plans. Instead, they brought school teams together for action planning and used the talents of their own excellent teachers, rather than outside consultants, to provide training.

Some states reported that the expanded responsibilities of SEAs helped them attract new talent who brought fresh ideas on ways to develop collaborative relationships with districts and communicate with local leaders and teachers. For example, Massachusetts hired former superintendents, who had positive track records of working at the local level and understood the challenges of translating state policies into practice, to support implementation of Race to the Top initiatives.

SEAs were also challenged to improve collaboration within their agencies between offices that traditionally functioned independently and were unaccustomed to sharing information or expertise. SEA leaders had to break down these internal barriers and establish a culture in which information was freely shared.

**Source:** US Department of Education.

Consultations on matters affecting teacher policy also need to include such groups as teachers' educators, employers and students. Box 3.5 outlines the range of consultation structures used in Hungary and Box 3.6 provides an example from the United Kingdom.

### Box 3.5 **Consultation structures in Hungary**

Hungary uses various mechanisms of dialogue and consultation to provide professional and civil society organisations with opportunities to present their interests in teacher policy reforms. The National Public Education Council (*Országos Köznevelési Tanács*) has the right to initiate and propose actions and to formulate opinion on the issues concerning education (e.g. regulation of syllabus, course books, teaching equipment, examination system, in-service training of teachers). The Council's agreement is mandatory for some decisions on public education. Its members include representatives of teachers' professional organisations, teacher-education institutes, the Hungarian Academy of Sciences, employers' associations and chambers, individuals delegated by the Minister of Education. The National Minority Committee (*Országos Kisebbségi Bizottság*) vested with similar rights in the education of minorities; all national minority self-governments delegate one member to the committee. The Council of Public Education Policy (*Közoktatáspolitikai Tanács*) acts for the Minister of Education as a board for preparing decisions, forming opinions and making proposals. It deals with every issue related to public education policy (except employer–employee relations). All significant professional, social and government partners are represented on this board, which is organised at the national level. The National Council for Students' Rights (*Országos Diákjogi Tanács*) may submit proposals on decisions pertaining to students' rights. It consists of nine members – three are delegated by the minister, three by the national student organisations for students between the ages of 6 and 14, and three by the student organisations for students between the ages of 15 and 18. Other consultative and policy bodies are concerned with tripartite issues between education-sector unions, education employers, and the relevant ministries, and the operation of vocational education and training.

**Source:** OECD (2005).

### Box 3.6 **The Civil Service Reform Plan in the United Kingdom**

The Civil Service Reform Plan (2012) outlines the UK government's aspirations to ensure that the government gathers evidence and insight on policy from external experts. Government departments across the United Kingdom use an official consultation process to help stakeholders engage, own and commit to policies, understand possible unintended consequences of a policy, and better shape implementation.

For example, the Department for Education in **England** (DfE) used the consultation process to gather proposals to reform secondary school accountability (2013) and make schools accountable for their pupils' progress across a broader range of subjects, instead of only on students' performance in the General Certificate of Secondary Education (GCSE). DfE received 412 written responses to the accountability consultation; it also held discussions with stakeholders at a series of events and conferences. Building on the results of the consultation, DfE designed a new set of accountability measures related to the performance-based tables to be developed from exam results. They will be used starting in the academic year 2015/16.

**Source:** OECD (2015).

### *Engage stakeholders and practitioners in designing and implementing policies*

The policy development process is more likely to yield consensus if policies are designed co-operatively among the different stakeholders working towards a common goal. Indeed, regular interactions help to build trust and raise awareness of the major concerns of others, thus fostering a climate of compromise. Evaluation policy, in particular, has much more to gain from forging a compromise among distinct perspectives than from imposing one view over all others. For instance, teachers will accept to be evaluated more easily if they are consulted as the process is being designed. The involvement of the higher education sector in innovating policies can be an important instrument too (Box 3.7).

### Box 3.7 German federal and *Länder* governments co-operate in the "quality initiative in teacher training"

The quality initiative aims to enhance the quality of teacher training at Germany's institutions of higher education. The goal of the initiative is to develop and multiply innovative concepts for teacher-training courses. Applications for funding from institutions of higher education are reviewed by education experts for the innovation and efficiency of their proposed projects. Funding guidelines have been agreed between the federal government and the *Länder*. The federal government is devoting around EUR 500 million for a 10-year period, beginning 2015, to support institutions of higher education in this way.

The "Standards for teacher training: Educational sciences" and the "Common content requirements of teacher training in teaching disciplines and subject-related methodology of the *Länder*" of the Standing Conference ensure high-quality teacher training at institutions of higher education.

**Source:** Standing Conference of the Ministers of Education and Cultural Affairs of the *Länder* in the Federal Republic of Germany.

If teacher-appraisal procedures are designed at the level of the administrative structure only, there will be a "loose coupling" between administrators and teachers that will both fail to provide guarantees of quality, and will discourage reflection and review among teachers themselves (Elmore, 2000; Kleinhenz and Ingvarson, 2004). Frontline actors, such as teachers and school leaders, may be in the best position to foresee unintended consequences and judge what is feasible in practice.

Involving teachers and school leaders in the development of education reforms is likely to facilitate the implementation of those reforms. For example, by engaging teachers in the design, management and analysis of students' standardised test results, teachers are more committed to the testing process and are more likely to apply the test results to improve student outcomes (Mons, 2009). Another example concerns the lead role to be played by teachers in developing and taking responsibility for teaching standards. Teachers' ownership of teaching standards recognises their professionalism, the importance of their skills and experience and the extent of their responsibilities (Hess and West, 2006). Education authorities also have a lot to benefit from experienced teachers providing advice on the design of teacher-appraisal systems. Based on their own experience and research, they are in a good position to identify effective teaching practices and to help develop relevant criteria and instruments to evaluate teachers (Ingvarson et al., 2007). As a result, factors that influence the success of introducing an evaluation system include professionals' acceptance of the system and perceptions of whether the evaluation processes are useful, objective and fair; and the extent to which evaluators and those being evaluated share a common understanding of evaluation purposes, procedures and uses.

Various researchers have stressed the importance of both, including the voices of stakeholders and professionals in the evaluation design process, and including stakeholders and professionals in the evaluation procedures, as a precondition for establishing trust and collaboration (Clifford and Ross, 2011; Leon et al., 2011). Studies by Thomas et al. (2000) and Davis and Hensley (1999) on school leader and evaluator perceptions of school leader appraisal in Alberta, Canada, and California, United States, respectively, revealed substantial differences between both groups, which provides some evidence for the importance of including school leaders in all stages of the process of developing appraisal systems as well as in the appraisal process itself.

The involvement of teachers and school leaders in their own appraisal process has been identified as key to the successful implementation of individual appraisal processes. Engaging teachers and school leaders in their own appraisal, e.g. through setting objectives, self-appraisal and the preparation of individual portfolios, can help create a more effective and empowering process for teachers and school leaders, and, therefore, aid successful implementation.

Teachers who are constrained in ways likely to reduce their own intrinsic motivation to teach may behave in more controlling ways and be less effective in teaching their students. By contrast, if teachers are involved in planning and implementing evaluation schemes, they are more likely to sustain reform efforts (Leithwood et al., 2000).

Several countries have established teaching councils that provide teachers and other stakeholder groups with both a forum for policy development and, critically, a mechanism for profession-led standard setting and quality assurance in teacher education, teacher induction, teacher performance and career development. These bodies aim to establish the kind of autonomy and public accountability for the teaching profession that has long characterised other professions, such as medicine, engineering and law. Box 3.8 outlines the development of the Teaching Council in Ireland.

### Box 3.8 The Teaching Council in Ireland

The Teaching Council, established in 2006, seeks to promote and maintain best practices in the teaching profession and in teacher education and training. As a statutory body, the council regulates the professional practices of teachers, oversees teacher-education programmes and enhances teachers' professional development. Through these activities, the council provides teachers with a large degree of professional autonomy and thus enhances the professional status and morale of teachers. The main functions of the Teaching Council are to:

- establish, publish and maintain a code of professional conduct
- establish and maintain a register of teachers
- determine the education and training requirements for teacher registration
- review and accredit programmes of teacher training
- regulate the induction and probation of teachers
- promote teachers' continuing education and professional development
- represent the teaching profession on education issues and establish procedures for exchanging information with teachers, organisations involved in education and the public
- advise the minister on such issues as: the minimum education qualifications required for entry into programmes of teacher education and training, the professional development of teachers, teacher supply and on the work of the Council
- conduct inquiries into the fitness of teachers and impose sanctions on underperforming teachers, where appropriate.

The Council comprises 37 representatives from various parties involved in school education: 22 registered teachers and 15 persons from teacher-education institutions, school-management organisations, national parents' associations, industry and business, and ministerial nominees.

**Source:** OECD (2005).

In addition to system-level consultative mechanisms and policy-making bodies, it is also important that teacher engagement occurs at the school level. Box 3.9 provides examples from Spain and Sweden.

### Box 3.9 School-level teacher involvement in Spain and Sweden

**Spain**

School-participation mechanisms are well established through a number of different bodies:

- *The School Council* is the basic policy-framing body and generally includes the principal, director of studies, teachers, students, parents, local authorities and non-teaching staff. Its responsibilities include developing guidelines for the overall school programme, the internal organisation of the school, the disciplinary regime, out-of-school activities and facilities management.
- *The Teachers' Assembly* includes the principal and the teachers. It is responsible for co-ordinating pedagogical decisions, such as defining student-assessment criteria, organising support classes for underperforming students, and providing counselling and guidance to students.
- *Co-ordination bodies* within the teaching staff complement school organisation. These include tutors, teams for different grade levels and pedagogical co-ordination committees.

...

  

**Sweden**

The principle of consensus is a central feature of the Swedish decision-making process. Dialogue and collaboration among various parties in the education sector is common, although it does not always result in consensus on changes in education policy. At the central government level, representatives of the Swedish Association of Local Authorities (SALA) and the teachers' unions often participate as experts in government committees or consultation groups on school policy. Stakeholders may also present their views through review bodies in connection with official inquiries and government proposals. Apart from such organised collaboration arrangements, various forms of talks and meetings offer opportunities for dialogue and consultations among parties.

At the local level and in individual schools, the Co-determination at Work Act guarantees that employers consult with employees before making major decisions about their workplace issues. Moreover, employee representatives concluded an agreement in 1992 that sets the framework for collaboration in the workplace. Under this collaboration agreement, employers and teachers seek to reach solutions on matters concerning workplace conditions.

**Source:** OECD (2005).

The need to more actively engage the teaching profession extends beyond reasons of politics and pragmatism. One of the main challenges for policy makers facing the demands of a knowledge-based society is how to sustain teacher quality and ensure that all teachers continue to engage in effective modes of ongoing professional learning. Research on the characteristics of effective professional development indicates that teachers must be active agents in analysing their own practice in the light of professional standards, and their students' progress in the light of standards for student learning.

Hargreaves (2003) has drawn attention to the difficulties of building collaborative cultures in schools, and of extending these beyond a few enthusiastic well-led schools and school districts. He argues that the approach adopted in a number of school systems amounts to "contrived collegiality", that is, collaboration imposed from above that "by crowding the collegial agenda with requirements about what is to be done and with whom, it inhibits bottom-up professional initiative ... As a result teachers sometimes actually collaborate less or abandon collaborative ways of working once the urgency of implementation or creating a school improvement plan has passed". He argues instead for the creation of professional learning communities within and beyond schools. Policy can encourage the formation of these communities through:

- leadership-development strategies that describe how to create and sustain learning communities
- building indicators of professional learning communities into processes of school inspection and accreditation
- linking evidence of commitment to professional learning communities to performance-related pay and measures of teacher competence used in recertification
- providing seed money for self-learning in schools and among schools
- professional self-regulation through processes and organisations that include all teachers.

### *Use and evaluate pilot projects before full implementation*

Policy experimentation and the use of pilot projects can help build consensus on implementation, especially as they allow for evaluations of the effectiveness of the proposed policies before they are fully implemented. Policy experimentation and the recourse to pilot schemes can prove powerful in testing out policy initiatives and – by virtue of their temporary nature and limited scope – overcoming fears and resistance by specific groups of stakeholders. A pilot implementation is a cost-effective way to ensure that a given initiative meets its intended purposes before full implementation. Seeking feedback from the involved school agents during the pilot implementation is essential for correcting the potential flaws and concerns related to the initiative being tested.

In Ireland, pilot projects are usually developed before wide-scale implementation. This is reflected in a school self-evaluation pilot project undertaken in 2010/11 by a sample of 12 primary schools in conjunction with the Department of Education and Skills. Similarly, the Project Maths initiative for second-level schools began in September 2008, with an initial group of 24 schools. Project Maths introduced revised syllabi for both junior and leaving certificate mathematics.

It involved changes to mathematics content, how students learn mathematics, and how they are assessed. The pilot project helped the National Council for Curriculum and Assessment (NCCA) to learn from schools how the proposed revisions worked in classrooms and led to the development of teaching and learning resources and assessment instruments (Irish Department of Education and Skills, 2012).

Another approach is to periodically review and evaluate processes after full implementation. Teachers and school leaders are more likely to accept a policy initiative today if they know that they will be able to express their concerns and provide advice on the necessary adjustments as the initiative evolves. Amsterdam et al. (2003) analysed the three-year development and validation of a school-principal appraisal system (i.e. standards, criteria and instruments) in South Carolina, United States, that involved researchers from the South Carolina Educational Policy Center at the University of South Carolina, the South Carolina Department of Education, a stakeholder committee (e.g. superintendents, school principals, teachers, guidance counsellors and journalists) and an expert panel. Superintendents responsible for carrying out the appraisal and school principals contributed to the development of standards and criteria through a survey and an online discussion group.

The new standards, appraisal criteria and instruments subsequently underwent a process of piloting and validation through focus groups. School principals involved in the pilot were surveyed to identify the strengths and weaknesses of the new system. Based on their findings, Amsterdam et al. argue that stakeholder input may help to ensure that appraisal systems are practical and useful for those concerned, and that the appraisal is supported by key stakeholders. At the same time, involving school leaders in the design of standards and appraisal criteria may help to establish an understanding of the criteria against which school leaders will be appraised.

In New Zealand, the Ministry of Education commissions independent evaluations to monitor the implementation of national policies. For example, implementation of the country's curriculum in English-medium schools was monitored by the Education Review Office (ERO) in a series of reports. The ministry, in collaboration with ERO, also developed a framework to monitor and evaluate the implementation of national standards. The "National Standards: School Sample Monitoring and Evaluation Project", run by a contracted evaluation team, collected information from a sample of state schools over the period 2009-13. This information was complemented by survey data, information from ERO reports and results from national and international assessments (Nusche et al., 2012).

In a range of countries, it is typical for external evaluators to collect feedback from schools and other stakeholders on their experience with the evaluation process in order to monitor its implementation. School-evaluation procedures may also be reviewed through national audits, stakeholder surveys, independent assessments and research studies. The same happens in the area of teacher appraisal. For example, the state of Rhode Island in the United States has developed a formal mechanism for evaluating districts' teacher-evaluation systems and using the resulting information to improve and validate those systems. The mechanism builds on a sophisticated set of standards that are used to guide the review of educator-evaluation systems. The results of evaluations are used to refine instruments and processes over time as new information is collected and analysed (Rhode Island Department of Elementary and Secondary Education, 2009).

### *Ensure adequate capacity and sufficient resources*

It is essential to develop capacity among stakeholders to implement evaluation and assessment policies. This includes providing support for school agents to understand evaluation procedures, training for evaluators to undertake their responsibilities, and preparation for school agents to use the results of evaluation. Evaluation and assessment are beneficial for improving education practices provided that they engage the skills and commitment of practitioners.

In addition, bureaucratic demands on schools need to be reduced and sufficient resources provided to implement evaluation and assessment policies. Both those who are evaluated and the evaluators should be partly released from other duties. Schools agents should have time to reflect on their own practices, especially when the process requires self-appraisal and the creation of a portfolio. The administrative workloads of evaluators, especially school leaders, should be reduced in order to provide evaluators with more time for evaluation activities, feedback and coaching.

Fiske (1996) underlines the importance of training policies for effective and successful implementation of reforms to ensure that all stakeholders are equipped and prepared to assume the new roles and responsibilities that are required of them. For example, for teacher appraisal, it is fundamental to provide in-depth training to evaluators to guarantee that they are legitimate in the eyes of teachers. Scepticism about the reliability of data stemming from a lack of capacity of schools and teachers to understand and use data to inform development is also likely to make it more difficult to implement these kinds of reforms (Campbell and Levin, 2008).

In Portugal, a variety of factors complicated implementation of a teacher-appraisal system in 2007: there was little experience with and tradition of evaluation; the system was unprepared to undertake large-scale teacher appraisal because of the limited professional expertise of those who were responsible for evaluating teachers; teachers complained that the system was unfair; excessive bureaucratic demands were imposed on schools; and little time was given to implement the model (Santiago et al., 2009).

In decentralised countries, where local decision making is pervasive, local education authorities often have limited capacity to implement evaluation and assessment policies. For example, there is considerable disparity in education expertise across Norway's 430 municipalities. Smaller municipalities do not benefit from the same capacity as larger municipalities to work on curricula and assessment reform (Norwegian Directorate for Education and Training, 2011).

Milanowski and Heneman (2001) found that even if teachers accept the standards of and the need for a teacher-appraisal system, they may still resist implementation if it adds too much to their workloads. And a study by Cullen (1997) on school-principal appraisal in England identified school principals' lack of time as one of the key challenges for ensuring successful implementation of the procedures.

### *Time the implementation of reform carefully*

As discussed above, not only is there a substantial gap between the time at which the initial cost of reform is incurred, and the time when the intended benefits of reforms materialise, but sometimes certain reform measures are best introduced before others, in a specific sequence.

Time is needed to learn about and understand the reform measures, to build trust and develop the necessary capacity to move onto the next stage of policy development. The World Bank distinguishes four phases of development of student-assessment frameworks, for example: latent (absence of assessment activity), emerging (enabling contexts, system alignment and assessment quality taking shape), established (enabling contexts, and stable, assured or consolidated system alignment and assessment quality) and advanced (enabling contexts and highly developed system alignment and assessment quality) (Clarke, 2012).

#### Box 3.10 The Alberta Initiative for School Improvement (AISI)

The Alberta Initiative for School Improvement (AISI) encourages teachers, parents and the community to work together to introduce innovative projects to meet local needs. The AISI was initiated in 1999 and it is now completing its fifth three-year cycle (2012-15). The AISI's platform allows schools and districts to develop teachers' professional capacity in curriculum and pedagogic development through its process of collaborative inquiry. Teachers in 95% of schools have been involved in continuous inquiry as a routine part of their professional practice.

The AISI was initiated and sustained through close partnership between the Alberta Teachers Association (ATA), the Alberta government and other professional partners, such as the Alberta School Boards Association. ATA is the single professional organisation to which Alberta educators belong and includes school principals and district (local authority) superintendents as well as classroom teachers. In addition to the typical collective bargaining functions, the ATA spends around half of its overall budget on professional development, education research and public advocacy for a stronger teaching profession, improved teaching and learning, and greater innovation.

TALIS 2013 clearly shows Alberta's strong commitment to teacher professionalism. Alberta teachers were more likely to report participating in professional learning than teachers in other TALIS-participating countries and economies: 85% reported participating in courses and workshops (the TALIS average was 71%); almost 80% participated in education conferences (the TALIS average was 44%); nearly two in three belong to a professional network (the TALIS average was 37%); and almost 50% were involved in individual or collaborative research (the TALIS average was 31%). Most Alberta teachers reported participating in professional learning, considerably higher than in other countries (4% of Alberta's teachers reported that they had never participated in professional learning compared with the TALIS average of 16%).

**Source:** OECD (2014); Alberta Education (2014); Hargreaves and Shirley (2012).

### *Build partnerships with education unions to design and implement reforms*

Putting the teaching profession at the heart of education reform requires a fruitful dialogue between governments and unions. A survey conducted in 2013 among 24 unions in 19 countries by the Trade Union Advisory Committee to the OECD (TUAC) revealed that many elements of this dialogue are already well developed.

The large majority of respondents to this survey indicated that they partially engage with governments to develop and implement education policies (Figure 3.1), even though just a small minority reported full engagement. However, unions considered themselves generally more engaged in policy development than in implementation. While most unions reported that governments had established arrangements for consultation, half of the respondents felt only partially engaged in these consultations. Fewer unions reported being engaged in consultations where formal structures for such engagement exist, compared to the willingness of governments to respond fully to consultation requests. That suggests that the mere existence of formal structures alone does not guarantee actual engagement. Perspectives sometimes varied between unions in the same country, reflecting the fact that governments may have different relations with unions representing different sectors of the workforce. Unions were also asked to identify areas of education policy that are currently the subject of productive discussions (Figure 3.2).

**Teachers' unions education policy engagement with governments**

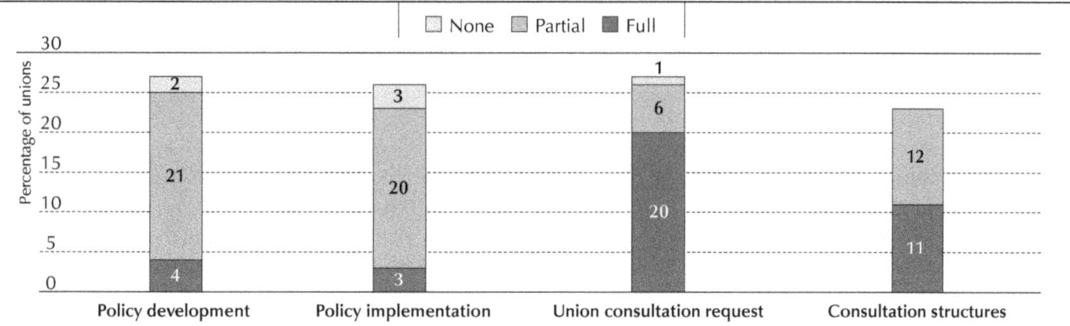


**Sources:** Data provided by Education International and TUAC (2013), Survey of Trade Unions' Engagement with Governments on Education and Training; OECD (2015), *Education Policy Outlook 2015: Making Reforms Happen*, http://dx.doi.org/10.1787/9789264225442-en.
**StatLink** http://dx.doi.org/10.1787/888933330569

Figure 3.2

**Teachers' unions/governments education policy engagement, by individual education policy**

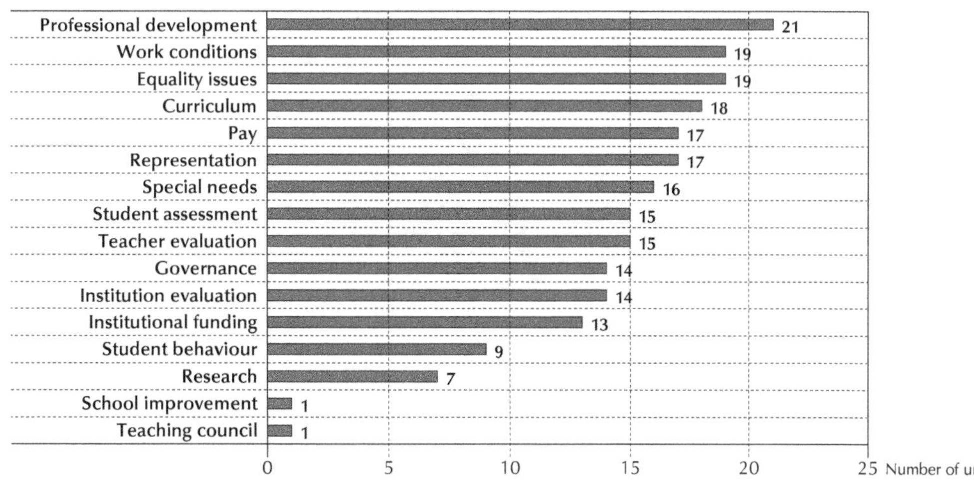


**Sources:** Data provided by Education International and TUAC (2013), Survey of Trade Unions' Engagement with Governments on Education and Training; OECD (2015), *Education Policy Outlook 2015: Making Reforms Happen*, http://dx.doi.org/10.1787/9789264225442-en.
**StatLink** http://dx.doi.org/10.1787/888933330576

Almost all respondents mentioned teachers' professional development, followed by working conditions and equity issues. Curriculum issues, pay, support for students with special needs, teacher evaluation, student assessment and institutional evaluation were also mentioned by a majority of unions. One-third reported productive discussions on student behaviour. Issues rarely mentioned were educational research, school development and teaching councils. Similar questions were asked about training policies (Figure 3.3).

Figure 3.3

**Teachers' unions training policy engagement with governments**

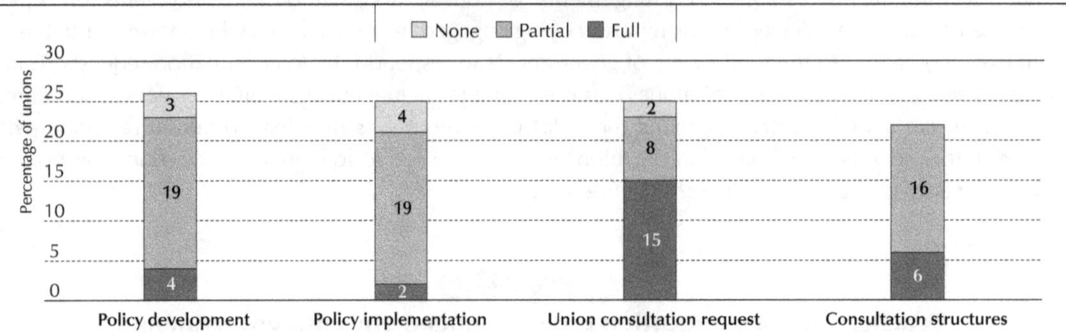


**Sources:** Data provided by Education International and TUAC (2013), Survey of Trade Unions' Engagement with Governments on Education and Training; OECD (2015), *Education Policy Outlook 2015: Making Reforms Happen*, http://dx.doi.org/10.1787/9789264225442-en.
StatLink http://dx.doi.org/10.1787/888933330587

While most respondents indicated that they were partially engaged with governments, more unions reported no engagement in implementing training policy than reported full engagement. Fewer unions reported that they were able to engage governments when they considered it necessary. While half of the respondents reported the existence of full consultation structures on education policies, fewer reported full consultation structures on training policies.

Figure 3.4

**Teachers' union/government engagement by individual training policy**

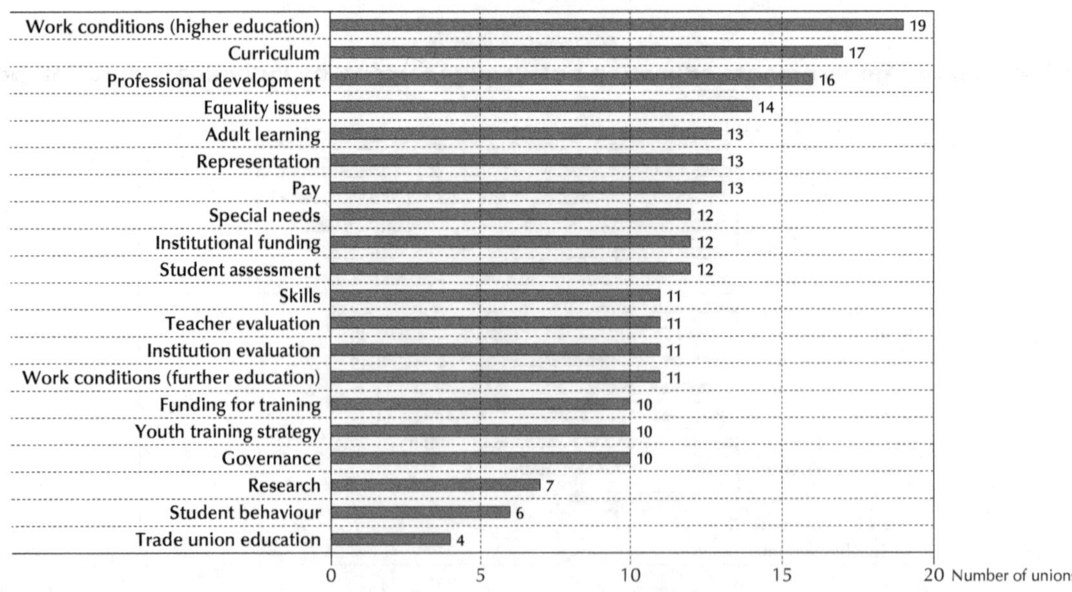


**Sources:** Data provided by Education International and TUAC (2013), Survey of Trade Unions' Engagement with Governments on Education and Training; OECD (2015), *Education Policy Outlook 2015: Making Reforms Happen*, http://dx.doi.org/10.1787/9789264225442-en.
StatLink http://dx.doi.org/10.1787/888933330593

Asked about areas of training policy that are covered in ongoing productive discussions, the majority of unions identified the curriculum, followed by professional development, equity issues, pay, adult learning and working conditions. Lower levels of consultation were reported for youth training strategies and funding for training (Figure 3.4).

In general, the TUAC survey presents an encouraging picture of union involvement in most OECD countries, particularly on teacher and skills policies. However, there is room for improvement in stabilising and institutionalising union-government dialogue. Examples of existing collaboration between teachers' unions and governments across OECD countries show that there are opportunities for unions to provide professional development and for teachers to share professional practice and leadership. Governments can recognise and support these initiatives.

## References

**Alberta Education** (2014), *Teaching and Learning International Survey (TALIS) 2013: Alberta Report*, Alberta Education, Edmonton, AB.

**Alliance for Excellent Education** (2010), *Principles for a Comprehensive Assessment System*, policy brief, Washington, DC.

**Amsterdam, C.E.** et al. (2003), "A collaborative approach to the development and validation of a principal evaluation system: A case study", *Journal of Personnel Evaluation in Education*, Vol. 17/3, pp. 221-242.

**Avalos, B.** and **J. Assael** (2006) "Moving from resistance to agreement: The case of the Chilean teacher performance evaluation", *International Journal of Educational Research*, Vol. 45/4-5, pp. 254-266.

**Blondin, C.** and **B. Giot** (2011), *Cadres d'évaluation en vue d'améliorer les résultats scolaires – Étude thématique de l'OCDE : Rapport de base pour la Communauté française de Belgique*, Ministère de la Fédération Wallonie-Bruxelles, www.oecd.org/fr/edu/scolaire/49048280.pdf.

**Campbell, C.** and **B. Levin** (2008), "Using data to support educational improvement", *Educational Assessment, Evaluation and Accountability*, No. 21, pp. 47-65.

**Clarke, M.** (2012), "What matters most for student assessment systems: A framework paper", *SABER – Systems Approach for Better Education Results*, Working Paper No. 1, The World Bank, Washington, DC.

**Clifford, M.** and **S. Ross** (2011), *Designing Principal Evaluation Systems: Research to Guide Decision-Making: An Executive Summary of Current Research*, paper prepared in collaboration with the National Association of Elementary School Principals, American Institutes for Research, Washington, DC, www.naesp.org/sites/default/files/PrincipalEvaluation_ExecutiveSummary.pdf.

**Cullen, K.** (1997), "An evaluation of the United Kingdom's national system of headteacher appraisal", *Studies in Educational Evaluation*, Vol. 23/2, pp. 103-130.

**Danielson, C.** and **T. McGreal** (2000), *Teacher Evaluation to Enhance Professional Practice*, Association for Supervision and Curriculum Development (ASCD), Alexandria, VA.

**Danish Ministry of Education** and **Rambøll** (2011), *OECD Review on Evaluation and Assessment Frameworks for Improving School Outcomes: Country Background Report for Denmark*, OECD, Paris, www.oecd.org/edu/school/47747224.pdf.

**Davis, S.H.** and **P.A. Hensley** (1999), "The politics of principal evaluation", *Journal of Personnel Evaluation in Education*, Vol. 13/4, pp. 383-403.

**Elmore, R.** (2000), *Building a New Structure for School Leadership*, Albert Shanker Institute, Washington, DC.

**Finlay, I., S. Niven** and **S. Young** (1998), "Stakeholders, consensus, participation and democracy", in I. Finlay, S. Niven and S. Young (eds.), *Changing Vocational Education and Training: An International Comparative Perspective*, Routledge, London.

**Finnish Ministry of Education and Culture** (forthcoming), *OECD Review on Evaluation and Assessment Frameworks for Improving School Outcomes: Country Background Report for Finland*, forthcoming at www.oecd.org/edu/evaluationpolicy.

**Fiske, E.** (1996), *Decentralization of Education: Politics and Consensus*, World Bank, Washington, DC.

**Flemish Ministry of Education and Training** and **the University of Antwerp Edubron Research Group** (2010), *OECD Review on Evaluation and Assessment Frameworks for Improving School Outcomes: Country Background Report for the Flemish Community of Belgium*, OECD, Paris, www.oecd.org/edu/school/46974684.pdf.

**Hamilton, L.** and **B. Stecher** (2002), "Improving test-based accountability", in L. Hamilton, B. Stecher and S. Klein (eds.), *Making Sense of Test-Based Accountability in Education*, RAND Publishing, Santa Monica, CA.

**Hargreaves, A.** (2003), *Teaching in the Knowledge Society*, Open University Press, Maidenhead, United Kingdom.

**Hargreaves, A.** and **D. Shirley** (2012), *The Global Fourth Way: The Quest for Educational Excellence*, Corwin Press, Thousand Oaks, CA.

**Hess, F.** and **M. West** (2006), *A Better Bargain: Overhauling Teacher Collective Bargaining for the 21st Century*, Program on Education Policy and Governance, Harvard University, Cambridge, MA.

**Hungarian Ministry of Education and Culture** (2010), *OECD Review on Evaluation and Assessment Frameworks for Improving School Outcomes: Country Background Report for Hungary*, OECD, Paris, www.oecd.org/education/school/50484774.pdf.

**Ingvarson, L., E. Kleinhenz** and **J. Wilkinson** (2007), *Research on Performance Pay for Teachers*, Australian Council for Educational Research, Camberwell.

**Irish Department of Education and Skills** (2012), *OECD Review on Evaluation and Assessment Frameworks for Improving School Outcomes: Country Background Report for Ireland*, OECD, Paris, www.oecd.org/edu/school/Country%20Background%20Report%20for%20Ireland%20-%20Evaluation%20and%20Assessment%20Frameworks.pdf.

**Keating, B.** (2011), *How Four Districts Crafted Innovative Principal Evaluation Systems: Success Stories in Collaboration*, WestEd, San Francisco, CA, www.wested.org/online_pubs/resource1109.pdf.

**Kleinhenz, E.** and **L. Ingvarson** (2004), "Teacher evaluation uncoupled: A discussion of teacher evaluation policies and practices in Australian states and their relation to quality teaching and learning", *Research Papers in Education*, Vol. 19/1, pp. 31-49.

**Leon, R.**, et al. (2011), *Key Features of a Comprehensive Principal Evaluation System*, WestEd, San Francisco, CA, www.wested.org/online_pubs/resource1107.pdf.

**Milanowski, A.** and **H. Heneman** (2001), "Assessment of teacher reactions to a standards-based teacher evaluation system: A pilot study", *Journal of Personnel Evaluation in Education*, Vol. 15/3, pp. 193-212.

**Mons, N.** (2009), "Theoretical and real effects of standardised assessment", background paper to the study: National Testing of Pupils in Europe, Eurydice Network, http://eacea.ec.europa.eu/education/eurydice/documents/thematic_reports/111EN.pdf, accessed 12 July 2011.

**Norwegian Directorate for Education and Training** (2011), *OECD Review on Evaluation and Assessment Frameworks for Improving School Outcomes: Country Background Report for Norway*, OECD, Paris, www.oecd.org/edu/evaluationpolicy.

**Nusche, D.** et al. (2012), *OECD Reviews of Evaluation and Assessment in Education: New Zealand 2011*, OECD Reviews of Evaluation and Assessment in Education, OECD Publishing, Paris, http://dx.doi.org/10.1787/9789264116917-en.

**Nusche, D.** et al. (2011), *OECD Reviews of Evaluation and Assessment in Education: Norway 2011*, OECD Reviews of Evaluation and Assessment in Education, OECD Publishing, Paris, http://dx.doi.org/10.1787/9789264117006-en.

**Nusche, D., G. Wurzburg** and **B. Naughton** (2010), *OECD Reviews of Migrant Education: Denmark*, OECD Reviews of Migrant Education, OECD Publishing, Paris, http://dx.doi.org/10.1787/9789264086197-en.

**OECD** (2015a), *Education at a Glance 2015: OECD Indicators*, OECD Publishing, Paris, http://dx.doi.org/10.1787/eag-2015-en.

**OECD** (2015b), "United Kingdom", in OECD, *Education Policy Outlook 2015: Making Reforms Happen*, OECD Publishing, Paris, http://dx.doi.org/10.1787/9789264225442-33-en.

**OECD** (2014), *TALIS 2013 Results: An International Perspective on Teaching and Learning*, TALIS, OECD Publishing, Paris, http://dx.doi.org/10.1787/9789264196261-en.

**OECD** (2008), *Reviews of National Policies for Education: Scotland 2007: Quality and Equity of Schooling in Scotland*, OECD Publishing, Paris, http://dx.doi.org/10.1787/9789264041004-en.

**OECD** (2007), *Evidence in Education: Linking Research and Policy*, Knowledge management, OECD Publishing, Paris, http://dx.doi.org/10.1787/9789264033672-en.

**OECD** (2005), *Teachers Matter: Attracting, Developing and Retaining Effective Teachers* Education and Training Policy, OECD Publishing, Paris, http://dx.doi.org/10.1787/9789264018044-en.

**OECD** (2001), *Learners for Life: Student Approaches to Learning, Results from PISA 2000*, PISA, OECD Publishing, Paris, http://dx.doi.org/10.1787/9789264103917-en.

**Rhode Island Department of Elementary and Secondary Education** (2009), *Education Evaluation System Standards*, Providence, RI, www.ride.ri.gov/regents/Docs/RegentsRegulations/RI%20Educator%20Evaluation%20Standards%208-06-09%20Public%20Comment%20Version.pdf.

**Santiago, P.** et al. (2012), *OECD Reviews of Evaluation and Assessment in Education: Czech Republic 2012*, OECD Reviews of Evaluation and Assessment in Education, OECD Publishing, Paris, http://dx.doi.org/10.1787/9789264116788-en.

**Santiago, P.** et al. (2009), *Teacher Evaluation in Portugal: OECD Review*, OECD, Paris, www.oecd.org/edu/teacherevaluationportugal.

**Thomas, D.W., E.A. Holdaway** and **K.L. Ward** (2000), "Policies and Practices Involved in the Evaluation of School Principals", *Journal of Personnel Evaluation in Education*, Vol. 14/3, pp. 215-240.

Chapter 4

# PROFESSIONAL TEACHERS, SUCCESSFUL REFORMS

This chapter summarises the key skills and attributes of 21st-century teachers, the most effective ways to develop teacher professionalism, and how best to design and implement education reform.

A generation ago, teachers could expect that what they taught would equip their students with the skills needed for the rest of their lives. Today, teachers need to prepare students for more rapid economic and social change than ever before, for jobs that have not yet been created, to use technologies that have not yet been invented, and to solve social problems that haven't arisen before.

Chapter 1 describes some of the broader expectations for teachers. At the level of individual students, these include to be able to deal effectively with students from different backgrounds and with different mother tongues, to be sensitive to culture and gender issues, to promote tolerance and social cohesion, and to work with students who have learning or behavioural problems. Teachers also need to be "assessment literate" and know how to use both summative and formative assessments. They need to be familiar with standardised assessment tests, to be able to use test results for diagnoses, and to be able to adapt their curricula and teaching in response to student achievement.

At the classroom level, teachers increasingly need to be able to teach in multicultural classrooms. More school systems are offering integrated education for students with disabilities and learning difficulties, and teachers are expected to be able to work with these students, use appropriate teaching and management processes, and co-operate with support personnel.

At the school level, teachers are expected to collaborate and work in teams with other teachers and staff members. They need social and management skills to co-operate, set common goals, and plan and monitor the attainment of goals set collaboratively. In many school systems, schools now use data gathered from self-evaluation or through testing and external evaluations to inform school-development processes. This calls for new skills in data gathering and analysis, and in communicating the results to parents. Teachers are expected to integrate ICTs into their professional practice and to keep up-to-date with ICT developments and applications. It is also becoming more common for schools to collaborate on joint projects and to develop links with schools in other countries. This means that teachers also need to cultivate their leadership and organisational skills, and their capacity to work and communicate effectively in a range of different settings. Last but not least, an increase in the number and range of decisions taken at the school level has led to new managerial tasks for teachers.

At the level of the wider community, school systems increasingly emphasise the importance of close co-operation between schools and parents. Consequently, teachers need to know how and when to communicate with parents. To gain additional support and offer broader learning experiences, schools are expected to build partnerships with community institutions and members, such as libraries, museums and employers. Teachers need to have the skills to make and maintain those connections.

Chapter 1 discusses the knowledge, skills and character qualities that teachers need to acquire to fulfil these demands. Subject-specific knowledge is generally seen as one of the main teacher-related determinants of improved learning outcomes. For example, while most international surveys of student performance do not find much of a relationship between the general level of education among teachers in an education system and student performance in that system, the share of teachers who have an advanced qualification in the subject they teach is often associated with better learning outcomes.

Pedagogical knowledge is important too. This knowledge of teaching and learning refers to the specialised body of knowledge concerned with creating effective teaching and learning environments for each and every student. It includes, for example, knowledge of how to structure learning objectives, how to plan a lesson, how to evaluate a lesson; knowledge of effective use of allocated time and strategies for differentiated instruction; and knowledge of how to design tasks for formative assessment. The knowledge also includes specialised areas of "learning", such as knowing how to facilitate learning given certain student characteristics, such as their prior knowledge, motivation and ability levels.

In sum, teaching is a complex task that involves interactions with a great variety of learners in a wide range of circumstances. It is clear there is not a single set of teacher attributes and behaviours that is universally effective for all types of students and learning environments, especially when schooling varies in many ways across different countries. That said, one consistent finding is that effective teachers are intellectually capable people who are articulate and knowledgeable, and are able to think, communicate and plan systematically.

## DEVELOPING PROFESSIONAL TEACHERS

Rapid changes in the demand placed on teachers, whether it is developing new skills or dealing with new student groups, imply that teachers can rely less on their initial training and need more continual professional development.



 

A comprehensive system for selecting, training, compensating and developing teachers and principals is important for building the required capacity at the point of delivery. Professional development can be achieved through apprenticeship, mentoring and collaborative learning environments. Much professional development is now school-based, led by staff developers who identify teaching-based problems or introduce new practices. This accords the teaching profession greater autonomy over professional development and facilitates a teacher-led culture of professional excellence.

To build teacher professionalism, policy makers and the profession itself must establish clearly and concisely what teachers are expected to know and be able to do. Such professional standards can guide initial teacher education, teacher certification, teachers' ongoing professional development and career advancement, and can be used to assess the effectiveness of each. The standards should be evidence-based and built on the teaching profession's definitions of teacher competencies and standards of performance.

Effective professional development is continuous. It includes training, practice and feedback, and provides adequate time and follow-up support. Successful programmes involve teachers in learning activities that are similar to those they will use with their students, and encourage the development of teachers' learning communities. A key strategy involves finding ways for teachers to share their expertise and experience systematically. There is growing interest in ways to build cumulative knowledge across the profession, for example by strengthening connections between research and practice, and encouraging schools to develop as learning organisations.

Three broad strategies for professional development are evident among the countries that participated in the 2013 OECD Teaching and Learning International Survey (TALIS):

- entitlement-based, which generally results from collective bargaining agreements that stipulate that teachers are entitled to certain amounts of released time and/or financial support to undertake recognised professional development activities
- incentive-based, which links professional development to needs identified through a teacher-appraisal process, and/ or recognises participation in professional development as a requirement for salary increases or assuming new roles
- school-based, which links individual teacher development with school-improvement needs.

The three strategies are not necessarily mutually exclusive, although the starting points of the entitlement- and incentive-based approaches tend to be the individual teacher rather than the whole school. A comprehensive approach to professional development encompasses all three strategies. Providing teachers with agreed levels of released time or financial support for professional development is an explicit recognition of the importance of professional development and a way of enabling teachers to participate. But it is also important for teachers to see the value of participating, to understand that it is an important part of their professional role, and to see the "entitlement" provision as the minimum extent of their participation rather than the maximum. This is most likely to occur when teachers can see a clear link between professional development activities, improvements in their own practice, student progress, and overall school improvement.

The most effective forms of professional development seem to be those that focus on clearly articulated priorities, provide ongoing school-based support to classroom teachers, deal with subject-matter content as well as instruction strategies and classroom-management techniques, and create opportunities for teachers to observe, experience and try new teaching methods. Effective professional development activities also forge a close connection between teachers' own development, their teaching responsibilities and their school's goals.

Encouraging schools to become learning organisations requires that teachers have: the *motivation* to create new professional knowledge; the *opportunity* to engage actively in innovation; the *skills* to test the validity of innovations; and the *mechanisms* for transferring the validated innovations rapidly within their school and into other schools. Targeted professional development activities can be an important source of ideas and techniques for building these features in schools. Equally important are skilled school leaders who are able to build a climate of collegiality and improvement within schools, and systems of teacher evaluation and career development that recognise and reward teachers who innovate, share their learning, and help achieve school goals.

One way to draw on the expertise in the classroom to build professional knowledge is to involve teachers themselves. Inviting teachers to participate is also a way of recognising their professionalism, the importance of their skills and experience, and the extent of their responsibilities. Teachers who reported in TALIS that they were provided with opportunities to participate in decision making at school reported greater job satisfaction (in all participating countries)

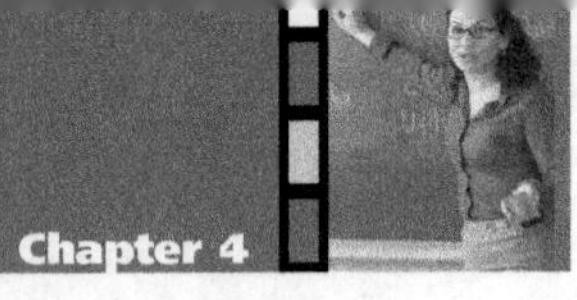



and a greater sense of self-efficacy (in most countries). The relationship between job satisfaction and teacher participation in school decision making is particularly strong in all countries. In addition, in almost all TALIS countries, the extent to which teachers can participate in decision making has a strong positive association with the likelihood of reporting that teaching is a valued profession in society.

Strengthening peer collaboration through induction programmes and mentoring is also important. The first years of a teacher's career can make or break that career. Induction and support programmes for beginning teachers can improve the effectiveness and job satisfaction of new teachers – and thus make it less likely that those teachers will leave the profession at the first hurdle. In successful programmes, mentor teachers provide guidance and supervision to beginning teachers in close collaboration with the initial teacher-education institution. These mentors provide on-the-job support, and identify deficits in subject-matter knowledge, classroom management strategies and other pedagogical processes.

Building a collaborative school culture is key. Chapter 2 provides many examples of how a collaborative culture can be created and nurtured. Evidence shows that collaboration among teachers enhances teacher efficacy, which, in turn, may improve student achievement and sustain positive teacher behaviours. Teachers in many countries are looking for more leadership opportunities – to lead change and not just manage what is demanded of them. By initiating improvement and innovation in schools, teacher leadership helps to develop teachers' competence and confidence as educators, advances their professional learning, promotes change and improvement in schools, encourages professional collaboration and collegiality, and boosts professional status and recognition. In doing so, teacher leadership helps to maintain and improve teachers' commitment, self-efficacy and morale.

It is also important to strengthen links between teacher appraisal and professional development. Teacher appraisal, part and parcel of effective teacher policies, will deliver best results if it is linked to professional development. In order for a vibrant programme of professional development to be established and sustained, it must be based on a culture of professional inquiry and on the professional obligation of every teacher to be engaged in a career-long quest to improve practice. A key objective of teacher appraisal is to identify areas for professional development for individual teachers. Ideally, this will lead to the preparation of individual improvement plans that take into account the school's development plan. Pedagogical leadership at the school level plays a key role in ensuring the effectiveness of this link. Identifying individual teachers' strengths and weaknesses is crucial for choosing from among a wide range of possible professional development activities those that meet individual teachers' own needs against each of the priorities in the school-improvement plan. It is important that teachers regard appraisal as the first step towards improved practice, regardless of their current level of performance.

## MAKING REFORM HAPPEN

Implementing education reform is difficult. Virtually everyone has participated in education and has an opinion about it; virtually every community has a school it can call its own. As a result, there are a lot of stakeholders in education who have a vested interest in maintaining the status quo. Even small reforms can involve massive reallocations of resources, and touch the lives of millions on both the client and provider sides. There is uncertainty about the size and distribution of benefits; and the issue of loss of advantages or privileges is of particular importance in education reform, simply because the vast structure of established (usually public) providers implies extensive vested interests. Not least, there is a substantial gap between the time at which the initial cost of reform is incurred, and the time when it is evident whether the intended benefits of reforms actually materialise. And while timing complicates the politics of reform in many domains, it seems to have a greater impact on education reform, where the lags involved are far longer than is typical of, for example, labour- or product-market reforms. As a result, the political cycle may have a direct impact on the timing, scope and content of education reform. Promoting education reform becomes a thankless task when elections take place before the benefits are realised.

But despite these challenges, education systems can and should be doing better. Both the lack of coherence in reform efforts across successive governments, and the fact that just one in ten reforms is subjected to an evaluation that makes any serious attempt to gauge impact are inexcusable and signs of a lack of respect for both taxpayers and educators at the frontline.

There are some basic features of education reforms that students, parents and educators should be able to take for granted. These include clarity of purpose and intended outcomes of reforms at every level of the system. They also include clarity about methods and delivery. Reforms should also include built-in means of public accountability – transparency in when and how judgements will be made as to whether implementation is on track and what the contingency plans are

when the intended results do not materialise. Last but not least, there needs to be clarity about the actors involved in implementation and their relationships. In other words, starting from the policy and ending with the changes in frontline behaviours and practices that this policy is designed to achieve, how – and through whom – does reform actually happen?

Beyond these basic features of reform design, Chapter 3 also examines some features for successful reform delivery. They include:

- a **shared vision**, clear and consistent priorities (across governments and across time), ambition and urgency, and the capacity to learn rapidly
- **performance management**, which includes appropriate targets, good real-time data, regular monitoring, incentives to reward success aligned to targets, intelligent accountability, and the capacity to intervene where necessary
- **frontline capacity,** which includes building professional capabilities, transferring and sharing best practice and innovation, flexible human-resource management, and frontline ethos aligned with whole system objectives
- a good **delivery architecture,** which includes strong leadership, effective interaction between links in chain, an evidence-based strategy, adequate process design and consistency of focus and prioritisation across agencies.

The chapter also identifies some challenges to implementation that are far more difficult to manage. In these cases, lessons learned from successful policy experiences across countries are particularly valuable.

First, there are few examples of successful and sustainable reform where policy makers have not been able to build consensus about the aims of the reform and engaged stakeholders, especially teachers, in formulating and implementing policy responses. The experience of OECD countries suggests that mechanisms of regular and institutionalised consultation – which are inherent in consensual policy making – help to develop trust among stakeholders, and help stakeholders reach consensus. And yet, there will always be tensions between the drive for ownership and consensus, on the one hand, and leadership and innovation on the other to achieve necessary improvements and transformations. When new policies are introduced, a combination of top-down and bottom-up initiatives is often needed. This combination can also foster consensus. Placing the teaching profession at the heart of education reform requires a fruitful dialogue between governments and unions.

It is also important that all political players and stakeholders develop realistic expectations about the trajectory of reform implementation, and the pace and nature of reforms. Teachers need reassurance that they will be given the tools to change, and recognition of their professional motivation to improve their students' outcomes.

Resistance to reform can be due to imperfect information, either on the nature of the proposed policy changes, their impact, or whether or not the stakeholders involved – including the general public – will be better or worse off at the individual or group level. All this makes it essential to clearly communicate a long-term vision of what is to be accomplished for student learning. Individuals and groups are more likely to accept changes that are not necessarily in their own best interests if they and society at large understand the reasons for these changes and can see the role they should play within the broad national strategy. The evidence base of the underlying policy diagnosis, research findings on alternative policy options and their likely impact, and information on the costs of reform versus inaction should all be disseminated widely, not just to the stakeholders with a direct interest.

The need to engage the teaching profession extends beyond reasons of politics and pragmatism. One of the main challenges for policy makers in a knowledge-based society is how to sustain teacher quality and ensure that all teachers continue to engage in ongoing professional learning. Research on the characteristics of effective professional development indicates that teachers must be active agents in analysing their own practice against professional standards, and their students' progress against standards for student learning. Policy can encourage the formation of collaborative cultures in schools through:

- leadership-development strategies that describe how to create and sustain learning communities
- building indicators of professional learning communities into processes of school inspection and accreditation
- linking evidence of commitment to professional learning communities to performance-related pay and measures of teacher competence used in recertification
- providing seed money for self-learning in schools and among schools
- professional self-regulation through processes and organisations that include all teachers.

Policy experimentation and the use of pilot projects can also help build consensus on implementing reforms, especially as they allow for evaluations of the effectiveness of the proposed policies before they are fully implemented. Policy experimentation and the recourse to pilot schemes can prove valuable in testing policy initiatives and – by virtue of their temporary nature and limited scope – overcoming fears and resistance among specific groups of stakeholders.

Equally important is to periodically review and evaluate processes after full implementation. Teachers and school leaders are more likely to accept a policy initiative today if they know that they will be able to express their concerns and provide advice on the necessary adjustments as the initiative evolves.

It is also essential to develop capacity among stakeholders to implement policies, reduce bureaucratic demands on schools, and provide sufficient resources. Training is essential to ensure that all stakeholders are equipped and prepared to assume the new roles and responsibilities that are required of them. Time is needed to learn about and understand the reform measures, build trust and develop the necessary capacity to move onto the next stage of policy development.

Together these challenges may seem large but this report provides plenty of examples of successful reform implementation and rapid improvement in the quality of student learning outcomes, which is the ultimate measure of success. These days, success accrues to those individuals, institutions and countries that are swift to adapt, slow to complain and open to change. The task for governments is to help their citizens rise to these challenges.

# ORGANISATION FOR ECONOMIC CO-OPERATION AND DEVELOPMENT

The OECD is a unique forum where governments work together to address the economic, social and environmental challenges of globalisation. The OECD is also at the forefront of efforts to understand and to help governments respond to new developments and concerns, such as corporate governance, the information economy and the challenges of an ageing population. The Organisation provides a setting where governments can compare policy experiences, seek answers to common problems, identify good practice and work to co-ordinate domestic and international policies.

The OECD member countries are: Australia, Austria, Belgium, Canada, Chile, the Czech Republic, Denmark, Estonia, Finland, France, Germany, Greece, Hungary, Iceland, Ireland, Israel, Italy, Japan, Korea, Luxembourg, Mexico, the Netherlands, New Zealand, Norway, Poland, Portugal, the Slovak Republic, Slovenia, Spain, Sweden, Switzerland, Turkey, the United Kingdom and the United States. The European Union takes part in the work of the OECD.

OECD Publishing disseminates widely the results of the Organisation's statistics gathering and research on economic, social and environmental issues, as well as the conventions, guidelines and standards agreed by its members.

OECD PUBLISHING, 2, rue André-Pascal, 75775 PARIS CEDEX 16
(91 2016 04 1P) ISBN 978-92-64-25204-2 – 2016

www.ingramcontent.com/pod-product-compliance
Lightning Source LLC
LaVergne TN
LVHW081418110826
845149LV00010B/1785